Failure to understand Australia's unwritten laws can lead to embarrassment, shame, ridicule and even suicide. But don't worry — help is at hand. This book is as much a humorous look at the Australian psyche as it is a survival manual to those trying to fit into this society.

Robert Treborlang has used his delicious sense of humour and gift of satire to pinpoint the frailties of the Australian ego. He has set himself the task of painting a light-hearted portrait of Australians, to keep like a family album.

He solves the riddle of Aussie etiquette, explains what makes Australians happy (bad sex), uncovers the rules of the national sport (splitting-the-bill), shows the importance of apologising (how to be sorry), explains the meaning of some classic Australian slang ("laid back" - an alcoholic who doesn't get violent), reveals how to be natural, and why European heterosexual men are like Australian homosexuals.

If you ever had difficulties in coping with relationships, family, friends or colleagues then this is the book for you.

Other works by the same author:

Books:
How to Survive Australia
How to be Normal in Australia
How to Make it Big in Australia
Sydney

Plays:
The Messiah in London
The Moon at Midday
Mr Mendelssohn Presents His New Oratorio "Elijah"
Obsessive Behaviour In Small Spaces (*with Ian Stocks*)
Fool's Gold (*with Ian Stocks*)
The Daisy Chain Gang

Poetry:
She Vomits Like a Lady

STAYING SANE
in
AUSTRALIA

ROBERT TREBORLANG

ILLUSTRATIONS BY
MARK KNIGHT

MAJOR MITCHELL PRESS

To Moi Moi, For Her Wonderful Heart

Some of these chapters first appeared in magazines and books and are reprinted through the courtesy of Major Mitchell Press from the following books: *How to Survive Australia, How to be Normal in Australia, How to Make it Big in Australia.*

First published October 1991
Reprinted November 1991
Reprinted January 1992
Major Mitchell Press
P.O. Box 997, Potts Point 2011
Australia

Copyright © Robert Treborlang

Edited by Derek Hornsey
Cover design by Mark Knight
Typeset in 11/12 New Baskerville
Keyset Phototype
Printed by The Book Printer, Victoria

National Library of Australia
Cataloguing-in-Publication Data:

Treborlang, Robert
Staying Sane in Australia
ISBN 1 875614 00 1

1. National characteristics, Australian.
2. Australia – Social life and customs
– Humour
I. Title

994.00207

Contents

Greeting rituals

Australians, a happy-go-lucky and gregarious race of fatalists, are still somewhat confused as to what greetings to use in everyday encounters. "How do you do?" — too stuffy. "How are you?" — old fashioned. "Good day" is all right, but unless pronounced with perfect inflection* it does more harm than good. "Hello" is not too bad, but considered weak. "Hi" — short but too informal. "Ciao!" is only acceptable to those who know how to spell it.

For this reason, the best way to approach and greet people is to pretend that your mouth is full of hard-boiled eggs or, even better, to wait for someone to greet you first, and then echo their own favourite expressions.

"How are you?"
"How are you?"
"Nice to meet you."
"Nice to meet you."
"Enjoyed talking to you."
"Enjoyed talking to you too."

Tourists and Newcomers usually have to struggle through a gamut of greetings before they realise that the society which has produced the corked hat and the wide-toothed shearing comb has not as yet created a greeting acceptable to all.

Which brings us to that other point closely involved in the business of greeting — the problem of living in a classless society.

In Germany, a nation known for its sharp class

*Several comedians and politicians have risen to prominence, simply for knowing how to say "Good day" with the correct emphasis.

divisions, the greeting "Grüss Gott" is acceptable to everyone from accountant to count. Similarly, in France, birthplace of snobbery, two men exclaiming "Ça va?" know exactly what class they belong to, but are prepared to overlook it for the moment. In the Soviet Union "How do you bear yourself, Comrade?" can be used freely (even if only one of the two present is actually a bear).

It's only in Australia, the classless society, that people's egalitarian spirit won't allow them to come up with a greeting formula which could be uniformly used. This needs explaining.

The Australian jealously guards the privilege to be considered the equal of all. However, the idea is that it is *oneself* who is the equal, not necessarily the others. Thus the Australian cherishes the idea of walking up to the Queen or the Governor-General and being able to exclaim "G'day" — while becoming most upset should someone else actually do so. If the Queen herself said "G'day" to an Australian, there would be a revolution.

Why you must always seem busy

Australians are generally very keen to impart the feeling that they've just been interrupted at something really important. This way not only do they appear busy but they are able to force the other person to act apologetic and tense, thus helping to keep up the level of anxiety all around.

"Oh. It's you."

"I am sorry, I didn't realise you were busy."

"No, no. It's alright. I suppose."

"You did say I should feel free to call in."

"Yes . . . That was on Wednesday . . . Before this thing . . . But it doesn't matter . . . sort of."

It is of the essence to understand that Australians are fascinated by the concept of being busy. Being busy is a sign of success. Not being busy is also a sign of success, but we'll go into that later.

To produce the best possible impression, Australians usually employ the following conversation. Remember — no matter what two professionals *might* need to talk about, it is much more important to discuss how busy you have been.

"Sorry I haven't called you for a while but I've been flat out."

"Oh. I wouldn't've had time to talk to you anyway. It's been absolutely hectic."

"Anyway, I couldn't've even considered talking. Haven't been so busy in years."

"Even if you did find some time, I've been up to my

"It's absolutely frantic."

neck in work."

"How could I? I've hardly had time to breathe."

"Not as frantic as I."

"You're joking! I was completely snowed under."

"Well, I was going mad!"

"Crazy!"

"Hysterical!"

But being *too* busy could be interpreted as trying too hard. Worse even — as being pushy and wanting to rise above those around you. So just in case, it's best to be well-prepared and carry the following dialogue to whip out on occasions when you might be thought overly ambitious.

"In fact this is the first chance I've had to relax."
"Same here. No good working too hard."
"No point running yourself into the ground."
"Man's only got one life."
"Must take it easy."
"Too much work makes Jack a dull jerk."

The idea is to appear always tense (from being busy) but in a relaxed kind of way (from not being busy after all).

"I know just how you feel."

Be sorry, be sorry, be sorry

Parents in Germany constantly encourage offspring to be thorough in everything they do. In the United States, kids are prodded to save whatever money they earn. In Japan, infants are urged to become loyal and hardworking. In Australia much of the time and energy spent on education goes into teaching children the importance of being sorry.

"Say you're sorry!"

"And what do we say now?"

"You better apologize or else!"

One can tell, in fact, sophisticated and well-brought-up Australians from the frequency with which they say they're sorry.

"I'm awfully sorry but..."

"I hope you don't mind that..."

"I regret to have to do this, however..."

In France, birthplace of courtly manners, should someone step on your foot it is socially quite acceptable to retort with something like: "Get off my bloody foot!" Such a statement in Australia just wouldn't be considered good enough. Properly educated apologetic Australians, if they say anything at all, would be expected to remark:
"I'm sorry to bother you and I hope I'm not too much

"I'm sorry to bother you and I hope I'm not too much trouble but could you move your foot a little either way because somehow mine seems to have got caught under yours."

15

trouble but could you move your foot a little either way because somehow mine seems to have got caught under yours."

Then, for good measure, you could also add (again):

"I really *am* sorry."

In this country you should never miss an opportunity to apologize. Do it under every possible pretext and with friends and strangers alike. You must say you're sorry especially: if you are right; if you think you might be right; if others agree that you're right; if you tell someone that you like them; if you're suspected of having made a mistake; if someone else makes a mistake; if you're getting drunk and falling over; if you don't happen to drink at all; if you happen to disagree with someone; if they disagree with you; if you are about to express an opinion; if you lose at a game; if you win at a game; if you haven't apologized for a while.

On arrival at an Australian home it's a good idea to start apologizing the moment you come in through the door. *Being on time* is a good excuse, i.e.: "I'm sorry to be so punctual." On being offered a drink you must excuse yourself for proving a bother, or better even, for actually being thirsty. It's advisable to throw in a few random apologies to keep the conversation going when sitting down, such as: "I'm sorry, have I sat on the wrong chair?"

It's also good form to be sorry for having burped. Even if it's impossible for other people to have heard it, you must bring your hand up to your mouth and stop all conversation with a loud: "I'm terribly sorry, it's awfully rude of me." In France and Germany, indeed, you might be thought gauche if you made such a statement. In Australia a bold apology for even the quietest little burp is considered the quintessence of courtly behaviour and your hosts will rush to have you over again.

Like religion, being sorry is something in which everyone must participate — a sort of chain reaction without end in sight. For example, it's important once someone apologizes to immediately apologize back.

"I'm sorry I took longer than I thought."
"Oh, I'm sorry, I should've realized."
"It's my fault and I'm sorry I didn't ring."
"I'm sorry then to put you to all this trouble."
"Oh no, I'm the one sorry for the inconvenience."
"No, no, it was definately my fault. So sorry."

Whatever you do, don't break the chain as it is considered both rude and dangerous. Unreassured apologetic Australians may even get aggressive. Australians who are not allowed to complete their apology become wild creatures indeed.

"I hope you'll forgive me for being late."
"OK."
"I'm sorry but it wasn't my fault."
"Good."
"I'll make sure it won't happen again."
"Fine."
"I said I'm sorry."
"I know."
"You don't believe me."
"I do."
"Listen, I can't do more than apologize."
"I understand."
"Well, if you're going to take that attitude, I'm sorry, but I'll have to leave."

Due to all these uses of the word "sorry", its actual meaning has somewhat changed. You must, therefore, *not* say sorry under the following circumstances: if you *know* you're in the wrong; if you know you've hurt someone's feelings; if you've made a mistake; when talking to somebody who has recently suffered a bereavement. In these situations the best line is always:

"I just don't know what to say."

The Old Mate Style of greeting

Advanced greeting rituals

Friends in Australia, meeting up after not seeing each other for a variety of reasons, and for periods that could stretch from a few hours to thirty-five years, always go through an elaborate ritual that is not necessarily known for its coherence.

It is important to study this rite, as you may be called upon at a moment's notice to join in. For men, it will very likely take place in a public bar, i.e. in the presence of males only — all initiates of the ritual exchange.

The Inarticulate Style greeting is conducted in a low key by two friends of any age. Let us say that you are former members of the same football club and now encounter each other about three times a year. As usual, it is in a crowded hotel.

"How's it going, Tim?"

"Great. How's it going, Tony?"

"No complaints."

"That's good."

"Keeping fit?"

"Just fine. And you?"

"Fair enough."

"Anything new?"

"Anything new with you?"

"About the same."

"Same here."

"It's great to see you."

"Great to see you too."

The ritual ends when you part, saying, "See you later, Tim", and "See you around, Tony", or when someone suddenly breaks into actual conversation. Then there is no stopping Australians until they have replayed every football grand-final for the past ten years and checked through every racing bet they intend to lay that weekend.

The Old Mate Style greeting is extremely loud and involves much vigorous back-slapping and punching on arms and shoulders, as well as a fair bit of shadow boxing. Let us say that two mates, meeting at a car auction, haven't seen each other since the previous sale.

"Hide the babes in arms! Look who they've let out of the desert! It's Dingo!"

"Stone the crows! Bluey! You old codger! Fancy seeing you here!"

"Crikey! Fancy seeing you! Getting any, mate?"

"Climbing trees to get away from it! What about you? Getting any?"

"Got to swim under water to dodge it!"

"You look as if you couldn't crack hardy!"

"No worries, mate! I've been so busy, I had to put a man on!"

"Same old Bluey!"

"Same old Dingo!"

This ritual continues until one says, "Remember the time we . . ." Then the real talking starts and goes on forever.

The Itemised Style greeting is practised by two people full of concern for their respective families, who cannot think of anything else to say. For example, two clerks who haven't seen each other since they spent the annual holidays together (in a caravan park in Queensland), might go through the following:

"Hi, Barbara. How's Phil?"

"Hi, Rose. Phil's arm mended just fine. How's Mike?"

"Terrific, Barbara. He's managed to rebuild the whole van. What about little Trent, got over his mushroom poisoning?"

"No problems. Peter and Kerrie got over their diarrhoea, I hope?"

"Right as rain. What about Tom's bronchitis?"

"Hardly ever wheezes these days. And how is Daisy?"

20

"Hasn't bitten anyone since. And how was your Mum's operation?"

"Great. Open heart surgery really agrees with her. What about your Uncle Bill?"

"He's fine too. They're just about to give him back his licence. And your sister Beverley?"

"Oh, great. Still on crutches, but looking forward to next year's trip."

When all the seats are taken.

How to avoid people

A cordial and friendly people average Australians seem to more than welcome you into their midst. This natural openness should not be abused, however, and you'd be well-advised to practise the restraint Australians clearly expect and deserve.

On trains and buses

Always sit on your own, as far away as possible from other passengers. This will show that you are both serious and self contained. Do not stare about you, fidget or hum in the manner of many overseas travellers. It's best to gaze at some unseen, inner landscape, as if in a trance.

Only when the entire bus or carriage is filled in this way is it permissible to sit next to others. You may now take a seat next to a stranger, but only with the utmost reserve and nervous uncertainty. *Ensure that no part of your body or clothing touches theirs.* Pick passengers not out of personal preference but because:

(a) they seem the least offensive; or

(b) they look as if they're about to hop off.

Standing in queues

Do not attempt to engage anyone in conversation while queueing up at a bank, a government office or some other public place. It might be acceptable to launch into a discussion with perfect strangers in Zagreb or Naples; many insecure Europeans, who've never met before, often end up having drinks together or beginning life-long friendships, simply through asking each other the time.

Australians, self-assured inhabitants of the world's largest isle, have no such immature habits and feel no need to communicate with strangers. On the contrary, since being singled out makes them feel ridiculous, Australians think it rather important to put unknown persons in their place and force them to realise that it is just what they ought to remain — unknown.

In the street

Should others approach *you*, the situation could be equally tricky. You're standing on a street corner, for example, with four of your girlfriends or mates. A well-dressed stranger with an open face walks up to you, wanting some information.

What are you to do?

1 Look quizzically with a frowning stare at your four friends who, all being Australian, will simultaneously return the same look to you. This long silent pause is essential to put the friendly stranger ill at ease.

2 Issue a series of non-lexical sounds as slowly as possible. "Um...gee...aaah...yeah..."

3 Pass the responsibility on to the person next to you: "Err...Ron, you'd know something about that..." (This well-rehearsed exchange is constantly practised in the Australian home, where Mum and Dad are always "passing the buck" to each other.)

4 Be very careful not to return the stranger's friendliness as that could embarrass your

Australian friends. The conversation, already staggering, should now collapse completely.

Remember that Australians in their childhood are told to beware of people, never to talk to anybody with too friendly a smile on their face, and to ignore those who wish to engage them in conversation. Sure, you might miss out on a few boiled lollies, but think of the successful way you can overcome some of the greatest perils of growing up in this country:

(a) finding out new information;
(b) making new friends;
(c) learning to cope with life through spontaneity and charm.

"Come on mate, I know we're climbing Everest, but it brings you bad
luck to prepare for anything."

Some Australian superstitions

Australians are a spiritual people with deeply held beliefs and superstitions, intent on warding off evil, bad luck and calamity.

Old World superstitions are: Never open an umbrella inside the house. Touching wood wards off evil. A pinch of salt over the shoulders keeps disaster at bay. Saying "Rain, rain, go away, come again another day" ensures bright, sunny weather:

Here are a few Australian superstitions:

1. Long term plans tempt fate.

You must always make short term plans because the long term plans won't work out. Like breaking a mirror and causing seven years bad luck, making long term plans might release malevolent forces. This is why at the mere mention of them Australians will screw up their eyes and utter in humble tones: "Who knows if I'll even be here in five years' time!" in order to re-establish the cosmic harmony.

If by some oversight Australians do get tricked into making far reaching schemes then they know it's best to ward off the inherent danger by immediately uttering incantations:

"Of course I am prepared to drop it any moment."

"I am a realist, I won't be disappointed if it doesn't work out."

"Let's face it, you could go out and get hit by a car."

2. You must never commit yourself to anything because it is sure to mean a debacle.

American, German and Chinese athletes get out there and tell you that they desperately want to break world records. They tell you this again and again, and often discuss in great detail what preparations they're engaged in to achieve their aims such as employing the services of a psychologist, embarking on some wonderful new carbohydrate diet, or practising an extra seventeen hours a day.

Australians believe that talking like this could prove dangerous and annoy the gods, whom they try to placate or propitiate by not discussing their true goals with anyone. If you feel that somehow you've been duped into admitting your real goals, or saying "I want to go out there and get this title, medal, record, and I will be very disappointed if I can't get it," it's a good idea to add quickly:

"Let's see what happens on the day."

"It's in the lap of the gods."

"I can only do my personal best."

Personal Best is the Australian equivalent of knocking on wood. As long as you say that you're doing your Personal Best you are averting the disaster of making the gods feel that you are too full of yourself.

3. Preparing in any way for the future spells bad luck.

Buying your funeral package can mean a sure fire catastrophe. "What happens if I die because of it?" or "What happens if I don't die?" Best to leave it alone.

The National Sport

In Italy the national sport is chasing the opposite sex; in Brazil, dabbling in *candomble* witchcraft; in Hungary, attempting suicide on quiet Sunday afternoons; in India, going on pilgrimage to remote and inaccessible temples; in the Soviet Union, dodging the secret police.

In Australia the national sport is splitting-the-bill.

Unknown in most other countries, splitting-the-bill is as uniquely Australian as the great rock of Uluru or the small perforations in Sao biscuits. Practised in the nation's restaurants, coffee lounges and hotels by people of all ages and backgrounds, bill-splitting is the embodiment of the Australian's personal commitment to fair play.

"Let me take care of this."

"Don't be silly."

"Ah, thanks."

"No, no, we'll split the bill."

The Chinese, by contrast, brought up under oligarchic regimes, do not accept the division of any restaurant account. Among them it is always the eldest at the table or the person responsible for the inviting, who does the paying. The Greeks too, warped by centuries of Turkish oppression, refute bill-splitting, and will fight to the last for the right to settle the entire tab.

Australians, unaware of their global uniqueness in this field, split bills on every conceivable occasion and as often as possible. With the single-minded devotion of those who know of no alternatives, they take the entire process rather seriously and practise with the fervour of devoted afficionados.

Like all deeply rooted indigenous sports, splitting-the-bill has strict rules which Australians learn from early childhood.

"I'm telling you, I didn't have the garlic bread!"

If you happen to come from an alien background, you might do well to practise at home and in small groups, until you're proficient enough to try it out in public.

There are several steps to follow:

1 Six good friends meet and decide to have a meal at an ethnic restaurant. All evening they remark how nice the place is, how good the food is and how cheap it is. Finally the bill arrives.

2 The bill is passed around and everyone studies the addition as if memorising it. No conversation takes place while this ritual occurs. Everyone is intent on the final outcome. Eventually a voice is heard to say:

"Twenty-two dollars each."*

3 You can be sure there's a few startled reactions:
"I didn't eat the garlic bread."
"But you had the mineral water."
"I didn't have a first course."
"You had some of my pancakes."
"But not the cucumber salad."
"*I* certainly didn't order it."

4 Details sorted out, the friends reach into their pockets and put some money on the plate. *Invariably the total comes to the wrong amount.*
"It's four dollars short!"
"It wasn't me."
"Me neither."
"Not me."
"And I haven't got my change yet."

Silence.

"We'll have to put in an extra 80 cents each."

5 Everyone throws down some coins and scurries away in a bad mood, before the waiter notices that they've left no tip.

---

* *One can always tell well-bred Australians from the speed with which they work out their share of a bill.*

How not to ask questions

In Europe, in the States, even in turbulent South America, when you wish to find out something personal from someone you simply attract their attention, look them in the eyes and say:

"Now, what exactly was your father's mother's maiden name?"

The European will immediately launch into an elaborate family history of the past twenty generations. The Yank will recount all the hardships his paternal grandmother had to endure during her early years on the Missouri. South Americans will volunteer not only their grandmother's surname but her twelve other names as well, along with the names of all her famous lovers.

In Australia, ask the very same thing and you will be considered the rudest person on Earth. Asking questions is the one thing a true Australian never does.

By wanting to know something, you immediately become suspect. You are also labelled a "nuisance" because you are an effort to be with. It will also be considered that you are after personal gain.

Let's say you are having lunch with some new friends at the factory cafeteria or at the office where you have found employment. Excited and curious, you decide to get things going by making what you believe to be innocuous conversation*.

> YOU: What do you folks do on weekends?

> THEM: (An embarrassed silence and interchange of looks followed by an outbreak of mysterious unease)

In Australia, there is no such thing as innocuous conversation.

Without knowing it, you have just made the following thoughtless allegations:

1 What gay bars do you frequent?

2 Don't your Alcoholics Anonymous meetings interfere with your weekend social life?

3 Do you happen to own a truck that could help me move my things on Sunday?

You are then likely to experience contorted mumbles due to mouthfuls of food, hurried excuses to leave the table, and glacial greetings for the next six months.

The Australian may want to know things, of course; curiosity is no less a human trait on the Lucky Isle than anywhere else. Australians may even be dying to find something out — but would certainly not dream of being so foolish as to allow natural instincts to take charge and permit the self-indulgence of actually asking.

What a successfully moulded Australian *would* say, when inquisitive, is:

"I understand from Jim Macleay that your grandmother was an Osborne girl."

To which the acquaintance will calmly answer: "No, no, you've got it wrong".

"Oh, I am sorry. I meant of course to say — a Chisholm."

"Wrong again", says the acquaintance with a twisted smile.

Confident that there are not more than two million names on any state's electoral list, resilient Australians will assume — quite correctly — that as long as they keep on trying, they must eventually get it right.

Of course, the alternative is not to ask anything in the first place — which is clearly what everyone has been doing all along.

This phobia about being asked questions remains to this moment a national trait which not even those practising it know about. Mention the topic to anyone and they will

34

look away, as if you have suggested that Australians might hide a mystery or two in their backgrounds.

To be fair, however, it does not require too much to convince the average Australian that they are rather irritatingly sensitive to questions. They will accept what you say — then simply not talk to you for a long time. Eventually, they are likely to greet you one day with an aggressive:

"Why did you say that?"

To this sort of question, of course, a reply is not expected.

Overseas people ask questions because they want to know the answers. In Australia, you ask questions only when you don't.

Never appear worried

To be normal in Australia you must never appear to worry about anything. Jovial and carefree, Australians pride themselves in being able to remain optimistic even in the face of the greatest adversity.

It may be acceptable to worry in Greece, Italy, or Yugoslavia. Nobody disputes the state of pessimism that rides roughshod over those lands. But in Australia, a young and vital nation, it is your duty to be nonchalant at all times. Everyone must deny any concern or emotional involvement, no matter what the situation.

"It's got nothing to do with me."

"I can't be bothered."

"Things always sort themselves out."

This attitude should be carried into all walks of life, especially road accidents. The instant you see one, rush over with the greatest possible speed, join the already growing crowd of idle observers, force your way to the front and make your optimistic views clearly known.

"He'll be right."

"I've seen much worse."

"It's only a surface wound."

"Doctors can do wonders these days."

"Reckon they'll have those legs sewn back in no

"A bit of physio and he'll be up and running."

time at all."

"A bit of physio and he'll be up and running."

"You hear that, mate? Mate? Mate?"

Take care, however. Under no condition are you to touch, help or move the victim, since that is the job of the proper authorities (anyone with a badge). Besides, should you do the wrong thing, you'll probably end up getting sued.

Your job is merely to be positive and reassuring.

There *are*, of course, the occasional pessimistic on-lookers with a compulsion to rush in, attend to the victim and race him or her to medical attention under their own steam. It goes without saying that these are negative thinking individuals who always assume the worst. Luckily their numbers are fast dwindling due to the realisation that too much initiative is really un-Australian.

Being cheery and worry-free is one thing, of course. Accusing others of worrying is another. Be careful never to say "You look worried, mate", or "Stop worrying" to an Australian, because that's how you start an argument.

"Frankly, I wouldn't worry."

"Who's worried?"

"Some people worry a lot."

"Not me, I never worry."

"I certainly don't."

"Well, I don't either."

"Why should I worry?"

"There's nothing to worry about."

In fact, saying "you look worried" to someone in Australia is tantamount to perpetrating a personal attack on them. By ascribing to people as much as a hint of worry, you've virtually accused them of:

(a) not being able to cope

(b) having failed the Australian jollity test

(c) being in need of psychiatric counselling

Should someone accuse *you* of being worried, or worse still, of *looking* worried, it's vital to demonstrate right away that you're nothing of the sort:

1 Scowl affronted as if they had said that your breath smells.

2 Talk about all the other people you know who have *real* worries — dob in everybody you can.

3 Sink low in your seat as if you're about to nod off, to show how relaxed you are.

Always project a worry-free image.* Act as if concern is the furthest thought from your mind. In fact, the worse things are, the more light-hearted you ought to appear.

Remember, in Australia, the only worrying you should do is never to appear worried.

*It's alright, however, to worry about numbers, i.e.:
"Did I drink 4 or 5 beers at lunchtime?"
"Will I back the 3rd in the 4th at Doomben?"
"I wonder which of the 6 plugs is misfiring?"

A note of caution

The Olde Worlde habit of coming straight out with a request is not going to be effective in a society that disapproves of questions. The Continental saying, "So shy she wouldn't ask the time of day", just does not apply to life in Australia. Here the less you ask for a thing directly, the more likely you are to get it.

It's best, therefore, to go around with a determined air of self-sufficiency, never letting anyone know what you are after. The very admission of a request puts the other person in an awkward position, i.e. they might have to do something about it.

Primitive and unsophisticated exchanges in places like Naples or Gdansk, based on the old question and answer formula, are over in a few short bursts:

"Why don't you ever take me out on your boat?"

"Haven't the time!"

"Won't you take me out just once for a few hours?"

"Alright! Alright! Tomorrow at seven?"

"Great!"

Contrast this with the profound exchange which Lucky Islanders have developed over many generations.

"Nice day."

"Yeah."

"I thought you'd be out on your boat."

"Too much trouble."

"I wonder what it would be like owning a boat."

"Oh. It's a lot of hassle."

"Yeah. I wouldn't mind buying one though."

"You should try mine."

"I'm not sure I'd have the time."

"You'd love it. I might take you out tomorrow."
"I couldn't manage it earlier than seven."
"Right. Seven it is then."
"Oh, my car's in dock at the moment."
"Pick you up on the way."
"Great."
As you can see, an example of perfect understanding using neither question marks nor changes in intonation.

Transaction rituals

Australians take great pride in their open style of business dealings and consider themselves world leaders in the field of honest transactions. Job interviews, commercial dialogues as well as business discussions in Australia are straightforward events that unfold in a most informal manner.

It would be a mistake, however, to take this congenial and open manner for granted. Australians may appear to be unaffected and casual but wherever they meet, be it in offices, pubs, clubs or television interviews, they perform several distinct ceremonial manoeuvres in the manner of mating bower birds.

The One-of-the-Boys style transaction consists of treating all prospective clients, bosses, employees or partners as if they have just arrived from Oodnadatta. The essential step here is to pay no heed whatsoever to the other person's likes, interests, biases or fears. People from overseas face some serious spiritual and bodily bruising unless they quickly learn to adjust to the terms of intimacy, first-name address, rib-punching, back-hand slapping and merry ridicules that accompany such transactions.

"No flies on you, Wolfgang, you bastard!"

"Aw, give it a go, Sadahiko, get that down your gizzard."

"Not a bad possie, eh mate, Mahmoud?"

It's useful to understand that the general aim here is

to impress upon everybody that all people are basically much the same but especially so in Australia. The exchange often takes place at a race track or nightclub on company expense and the interchange continues until one of the parties feels violently ill or collapses completely.

The Full On style is practised by Australians who behave in an overly aggressive manner in order to disguise uncertainty about what exactly people want or are after. Exchanges that you might adopt in the course of such encounters are:

"I'm awake-up to you, matey."

"Come on, stop bunging on an act."

"I didn't come down in the last shower."

"You couldn't knock the skin off a rice pudding."

"What do you think you're trying to pull?"

"You couldn't give away blood at a lice picnic."

"Well, I reckon you're up shit creek without a paddle."

"You're lower than a worm's belly."

"You're as shady as a rat with a parasol."

The Full On style serves to slowly pump confidence into all parties concerned while giving them time to think.

The Devil's Advocate style consists of permanently taking up a contrary position to the other person. One party always opposes whatever the other one is saying, in the name of Truth. Practised particularly by members of the media, the Devil's Advocate style proves that neither bias nor favouritism tinges your judgment.

"I've just discovered a cure for cancer."

"Have you thought of the consequences?"

"I beg your pardon?"

"The doctors, nurses and other staff you'll put out of work?"

"Well, actually..."

"The technicians and hospitals out of action?"

"Steady on..."

"The morticians and lawyers who will go broke?"

"But the world's been seeking the cure for centuries!"

"I suppose you did it on a grant, eh?"

The Excessively Friendly style is practised by Australians from all walks of life interviewing aspiring candidates for positions vacant, for tenders or grants, for bank loans or for partnership offers. The procedure involves a lot of sympathetic body language, quiet conspiratorial asides and little verbal nudges.

"Yeah, your prospects look pretty good."

"I think you're really suited for the job."

"I'll certainly be pushing your cause."

Should you encounter such behaviour, beware immediately that you have made an unfavourable impression. Interviewers most likely think you pushy. The moment the atmosphere becomes matey, relaxed and informal, you can be fairly sure that your prospects are slim indeed. The job is definitely going to someone else. You certainly haven't got that contract. In fact you're not even in the race.

The Aloof style is a stiff manner employed when holding interviews, board meetings, staff meetings and grant applications. Movements are jerky, eyes are averted and the voice is hollow.

"I don't think you understand the situation."

"I'm afraid I don't agree with you."

"You're wrong there."

In Europe such contentious remarks are a fairly good indication of the futility of a situation. Aloof behaviour on the part of your basically easygoing Australians simply means that you have made an excellent impression, that you may be fairly sure of landing that uncertain contract, or that a promotion is most likely coming your way.

Do not fall into the trap of trying to be amicable. Make sure you don't try to warm up the situation with any friendliness. To the trick question "Any questions?" make sure you do not answer anything, shrug your shoulders and stare out the window.

In this situation ensure that there is no eye contact whatever. In Australia the only people who look their employers in the eyes are desperate ones.

The Difficult Beginnings style of exchange is very common in Australia and takes place between two people who wish to do business together, but at first are scared of each other. Then as the meeting wears on you warm up to one another.

"Hey, you're not a bad bloke/sort/person."

"You're not so bad yourself."

"I think we could do business together."

"I'm sure we could."

"We'll get on great guns."

"Like a house on fire."

"Like fleas on a bandicoot."

"We'll show 'em."

"My oath."

The exchange continues until you are so comfortable in each other's company that you can skip the business part altogether and go out instead and have a beer.

What makes Australians happy?

Bad sex, for one.

For the female it gives her a central issue around which to revolve all her emotional life. And it gives her a good excuse to test as many men as she likes.

For a man bad sex is terrific. It gives him lots of time to drink with his mates; he can ignore women; stay out late; spend all his money on himself, and punt a fortune at the track.

Good sex has a tendency to go bad anyway. Bad sex can't get worse, of course, but gives you the freedom to gossip with close friends and motivates you to join physical fitness classes or start a new career.

Natural Disasters.

They help unite everyone and make you feel close to people you don't know and never will. You can happily clear out all the junk that has accumulated in the garage over the last ten years and know that you are donating the inappropriate stuff to a worthy cause.

Coming second last.

Obviously you've done your personal best and haven't come last so you're not completely hopeless.

You don't have to deprive yourself with endless hours of training and pep talks which would be necessary in order to come first.

You don't have to feel envious of the winner which would be natural if you came second.

And by not coming third you spare yourself the irritation of thinking that if only you had strived a little harder you might have got silver.

You also don't have to make endless excuses of why you finished back in the field because now you can say: "At least I didn't come last! Ha! Ha! Ha!"

What a happy state this is.

First, Second, Third and Personal Best.

How to be passive

Whilst in Europe, Asia and America men without initiative might be shunned, avoided or even ostracized, in Australia this quality is actively sought out, recognized and encouraged by every sensitive and romantic woman.

What elegance and *savoir faire* do for French girls, or bareback yak hunting does for Tibetan beauties, showing lack of initiative does to the Australian female.

To Europeans, indeed, the attraction Australian women feel for men who sit in corners all night, staring at their nails, or who gaze wistfully at wallpaper patterns, may seem slightly eccentric. To the Japanese the penchant of the Australian female for making the first move towards a relationship might even seem pushy. To South Americans, not unexpectedly, the Australian male's habit of waiting to be spoken to would seem rather unexciting.

Australian males, of course, know better. They understand only too well that the less energy they expand and the more passive they behave, the greater their chances of being picked up. They know that women have to be allowed to take the initiative, otherwise things would never get anywhere. After all, there's nothing Australian females suspect more than a man going out of his way to make an impression.

"He likes you."

"He's a creep."

"What's he done?"

"Keeps on telling me how much he likes me."

I discovered the importance of acting passive at my very first Australian party. Around midnight I began to notice that guys who, till then, had sat around in corners and never paid the slightest attention to anyone or anything all night, were now approached by girls who had spent the whole time chatting to each other.

"You're very quiet."

"I'm alright."

"You don't seem to be enjoying yourself."

"I'm not a party person."

"Neither am I really."

"I like to get to know people one at a time."

"Why don't we go outside then?"

"Alright."

I realised that Australian women were strong-minded, proud individuals who would hate the idea of someone deliberately setting out to seduce them. A man may entertain desires, he may even have designs, but they should not be revealed under any circumstances.

"What shall we do?"

"Up to you."

"A drive?"

"I don't mind."

"Where to?"

"I'm easy."

Since the aim is to protect the woman from feeling that advantage is being taken of her, and as even the most minimal difference of opinion could land you in trouble, further conversations ought to be limited to a few neutral topics. Any of the following will do:

- the trade-in value of cars

- the pros and cons of various alarm systems

- what sandwiches you have for lunch

- problems of people she's never met

Equally important is to be passive in a relationship. Should someone telephone, for instance, to invite the

How to be passive.

two of you, care must be taken not to show too independent a spirit.

"What are you doing next Saturday?"

"I'm not sure."

"Would you like to come to a party?"

"Wait till I ask Fiona."

In Germany or Russia it may be acceptable for a man to reply promptly "Yes" to an invitation. In Australia, however, it is the woman's prerogative only to pick up the phone and accept with a cheery:

"We'd love to come."

Failure to comply with the simple rules of passivity could rapidly escalate into circumstances beyond anyone's control.

"What did you do that for?"

"What's that?"

"Saturday was going to be my quiet night."

"I just thought..."

"Well, you can go on your own."

It's best not to reply. Sit on the edge of a chair or sofa and gaze crestfallen at the floor, until your partner relents.

And if you're passive enough, they will.

Why kissing always means "yes"

It's all very well for Italians or South Americans to kiss at the slightest pretext — flirtatious people by nature, for them kissing is a shallow affair. Many may even do it with people on whom they have absolutely no designs.

Australians, highly moral and honourable by contrast, will kiss for one purpose and one purpose only.

In Europe when two people get to kiss each other, they often perform the act in a passionate though not overly optimistic manner. Europeans as a rule kiss purely for pleasure, often using it to avoid deeper, more intimate commitments.

In Australia once you've kissed there's no turning back. Australians kiss to let you know that they're ready. Like now.

"Mmmm. That was nice."

"Yeah"

"Something just clicked."

"Sure did."

"Wait till I lock the door."

Kissing is the key ritual of an otherwise straightforward operation. Australians are meticulous about kissing and have made it the cornerstone of sex.

"Kiss me again."

"No."

"Why?"

"Let's make love instead."

After all, if you are going to go to all the trouble and

actually invade someone's personal space, you might as well go all the way.

Many people from overseas, after making initial contact with Australians and kissing them quite passionately, think nothing more of it. On the following occasion, wishing to pick up where they left off, these folk are shocked to find that they no longer arouse the same degree of interest as before.

"What's wrong?"

"Nothing."

"Then kiss me."

"What's the point?"

"I like you!"

"You sure didn't show it last time."

The most popular and successful lovers in Australia know to hold back to the last moment and not to waste their kisses on hellos or goodbyes. They know only too well that kissing must be reserved for the following occasions:

(a) as an indication of readiness;

(b) as a signal that the congress is over; and

(c) when you're drunk.

A successful romantic evening in Australia consists of not kissing on meeting, absolutely not touching during dinner, major physical reticence on the way home, total abstinence while sitting around before the TV set, not even a hint of physical closeness while you're having that last nightcap. Then, just as you are about to say goodbye and both are wondering whether perhaps the other one is not a bit funny, one all-exploding kiss must come as a complete and instant outpouring of tension.

Your highly reticent and moral Australian is now ready.

A modest observation

Men in Australia become homosexual if they like women and heterosexual if they don't.

This transcendental truth came to me early on when I made the acquaintance of a beautiful Australian girl. No sooner were we introduced, than she began to treat me like an old friend. She rewarded my compliments with little hugs, laughed at my travel adventures and in general acted wonderfully relaxed.

At the end of the evening I took her home. Seated on her sofa, close to each other, we continued telling amusing stories over a cup of coffee. Suddenly as she brushed close to me, I leaned forward and kissed the girl on the mouth. She tensed up, became stiff and pressed herself against the far edge of the sofa.

"What's wrong?" I said.

"I thought you were homosexual," she told me.

"How come?"

"You're too friendly to be straight."

"But you were friendly too!" I exclaimed.

"Because I thought you were gay!"

From that moment on the atmosphere changed dramatically.

The conversation was no longer easy-going and the girl behaved with an odd formality. No matter how affectionately I treated her, she responded tautly and spoke with long awkward pauses.

"Sure you aren't homosexual?" she asked again.

"Of course not."

Heterosexual.

"Only gay men act so relaxed with women here."

"Then how do Australian heterosexual men act?" I asked.

"*Nor*mal," she said.

After much trial and error, I discovered over the next few months that only when I too tensed up, acted gruff and spoke with long awkward pauses, did Australian women seem to take my advances seriously and accept me as a potential romantic partner.

I had stumbled upon the Australian *heterosexual mode* and uncovered two very important basic rules:

1. Gay men in Australia behave towards women with the same relaxed, easy-going attitude that heterosexual men manifest towards women in Europe. Brought up by righteous-minded mothers and aunts, homosexuals here have a deep respect for females and would rather regard other men only as sex objects. By contrast, and in order to be identified as heterosexuals, straight men in Australia have to act surly, tense and uneasy with women, as if they didn't like them at all. They must also look ready to bolt at any moment and run back to their mates.

Homosexual.

2 Gay men in Australia, when visiting their women friends, bring flowers, boxes of chocolates or champagne, much like straight men do in Europe. They are also the ones who entertain the women with amusing stories and flattering compliments at parties and in public places. Heterosexual Australian men, on the other hand, wanting to be recognised as such, have no choice but to slouch in corners and grunt into their drinks. Since they also consider taking presents when visiting rather cissy, straight men prefer just to bring themselves.

Sex by attrition

When Iraq and Iran went to war the whole world expected a quick end to the conflict. Instead the two countries settled down to a long-winded struggle with the aim of wearing down each other's resistance.

It's what is called a war of attrition.

If you want to be successful with the opposite sex in Australia, you must learn the art of attrition, as courtship Down-under is run along much the same lines.

Australians, you see, are independent and proud beings who consider that any admission of desire shows a demeaning lack of character. One may have urges, one may even entertain certain designs, but these should not be revealed under any circumstances. On the contrary, all references to real intentions ought to bring out a hot denial:

"I think you've got the wrong idea about me."

"I'm just not like that."

"It was the last thing on my mind."

Half-hearted excuses like "What's wrong with that?" and "Haven't had it for weeks" simply won't do. Even the slightest admission of desire can lead to untold complications and risks being seen like trying to extract sex from the other person.

"You're not really a bad sort."

"Thanks."

"I reckon you look a bit of all right."

"Oh yeah?"

"So, what shall we do now?"

"Actually I quite like you."

"I knew you'd turn out to be a creep."

It may be admissible for a Frenchman to sight a pretty girl in Montmartre, share a quick lunch with her and then, after declaring his intentions, end up having a siesta together an hour later. In Australia this kind of spontaneity is frowned upon and is seen in the same light as queue-jumping.

Australians are a well-brought-up moral nation who've learnt since childhood that you've got to take the bad with the good. After all, one can't just go from soup to dessert. And one certainly couldn't have sweets on its own.

"Finish your vegetables."

"But I don't want to!"

"Finish them!"

"Can't I just have dessert?"

"You'll eat your greens or go without!"

Successful Australian lovers, therefore, go out together for drinks, eat something, then walk around a bit, have a few more drinks, go to a movie, drive back to either one's place, sit around, play some records, snack, watch the late news, have another drink, sit around some more or read the papers and then, when they run out of all other possibilities, when there is absolutely nothing left to do, they go to bed.

It's sex by attrition.

Three games for beginners

Here are three amusing and very effective techniques for maintaining the optimum level of necessary tension with a partner, should you end up in an antipodean relationship.

Doesn't Matter

Whenever your partner comes into the house or you meet up somewhere, just stare into thin air with a vague expression. It is immensely satisfying to see them squirm as they try to find out what's wrong.

"You look upset."

"No, I don't."

"What did I do?"

"Forget it."

"I want to know."

"It doesn't matter."

This dialogue may be kept going until you get bored or your partner reaches breaking point.

Someone Saw You

If there's the occasional relaxed moment, never wait for it to be over. If you speak quietly and with good timing — and in Australia such timings are learnt from early childhood — the atmosphere will be instantly charged with tension and guilt.

"Someone saw you the other day."

"Really? Where?"

"They wouldn't say."

"Who was it?"
"I better not tell you."
"Why not?"
"You wouldn't like what they said."
"Why? What did they say? Tell me!"
"No, I better not."

This can go on for ever and is especially entertaining when you've made the whole thing up.

Us Really

Should your partner seem a little too happy or carefree, throw your head back, sigh, shut your eyes and tighten your lips.
"What's wrong?"
"I was just thinking."
"What about?"
"Us, really."
"What about us?"
"You wouldn't understand."

It is highly gratifying to see them tense up and start to worry. There's also a good chance they'll eventually develop an ulcer.

Classic Australian slang

It was a good team atmosphere: Nobody did any work.
He's in brilliant form: Will get knocked out before the finals.

She's a really nice lady: Inhibited or not very good looking.

Laid back: An alcoholic who doesn't get violent.

He knows his job: Doesn't know his job.

He's a male chauvinist pig: Won't pour your beer into a glass.

Knows everybody: Someone who grins a lot.

I work hard and I play hard: I am a failure.

He's a real Socialist: In the process of bankrupting both branches of the family.

Totally new and revolutionary: Appeared in America six months ago and now I am copying it.

Made in Australia: Origins unknown.

My best friend: I've been sleeping with his girlfriend for six months.

My best girlfriend: I've slept with all her boyfriends.

On a par with New York: Harlem, that is.

Australia is the best country in the world: I am very insecure.

It's of world standard: Third world, that is.

Biggest in the Southern Hemisphere: Quite big.

Innovative: There's something wrong with the design.

Second rate: Fifth rate.

How to be Low Key

Quintessentially *the* Aussie trait — especially when dealing with people.

Being Low Key is neither a mannerism nor a fashion. It is as basic to being Australian as rust is to motor cars, or grey fur to koalas.

Low Key has to do with pretending that you're a lot less than what others think you are (if this is possible).

Being Low Key also means wearing unfashionable clothes (see next topic). Remember at all times that the actual quality of the clothes in your wardrobe is not important. What really matters is that they should look as if they were meant for somebody else.

Low Key has to do with being awkward, clumsy and rather ungrammatical.

Achievements, assets, attitudes, should only be referred to with badly constructed . . . you know . . . lots of punctuation marks . . . sort of . . . obliquely . . . and how can one put it . . . Uncertain . . .?

Ambition must also be heavily played down and its hard-earned fruits should always be attributed to . . . err . . . Luck?

Low Keyness doesn't only mean being unable to formulate sentences about your own successes. It also means cutting off other people as they are trying to tell you something successful about themselves.

Low Key has to do with warding off envy.

Like the plumber who has just won a tray of meat at a pub raffle. He knows how to be Low Key, by instinct. And his mates, holders of the losing tickets, surround him with a twinge of envy, as he keeps fumbling with his prize.

PLUMBER: Yeah . . . yeah . . . yeah . . .
MATES: A tray of meat, eh?
PLUMBER: (Laughs nervously) Heh! Heh! Heh!
MATES: Last week it was turkey!
PLUMBER: (Sadly) But I like turkey.
(Nice uneasy atmosphere but at least nobody's resentful.)

Being Low Key also puts a nice reassuring gulf between yourself and those who might want to get close.
Like women.
Opening doors for the opposite sex is fine but make sure you get in the way as she is trying to pass you. Rush to offer her a lighter *after* she's already fished out her own. Farting in bed is OK too, but make sure you first let out an enthusiastic "Wait for it!".

Antipodean chivalry

How not to dress well

Overseas, people's clothes indicate the social class they come from. In Australia, clothes are meant to disguise it.

This transcendental truth came to me early on and quite by accident. I was taken along to the home of a wealthy land developer where, I was assured, I would meet rich and important people. I went to seek out my host and addressed the most elegant man present. It turned out he was the maitre d'. The second most elegant man turned out to be the pianist hired for the evening. The third best dressed man was someone's bodyguard. My search continued down the line, until finally I found my host: he was wearing the crumpled suit and battered shoes of a man who's come to give a quote on removing the vermin.

I expressed my astonishment, since back in Europe a rich man would rather kill himself than be seen in such an outfit. In Europe, elegance is an obsession. The concept of "everything he owns, he wears on his back" was devised to designate a large percentage of the continent's population. Europeans who don't look more than they are worth, get a raw deal indeed, and stories about such people are legion.

"The richer one is in Australia," explained my host, "the poorer he must dress, in order to keep the nation democratic. I know this may seem difficult to understand since Australia is such a free and affluent country, but you could visualise it in terms of being an escapee from Siberia, trying to make your way across the Soviet Union to the Norwegian border. At all costs, you would want to blend in with the environment, and wherever possible, disappear from view completely."

"So what is one escaping from in Australia?" I asked.

"Envy."

It was my first lesson in being Low Key.

Not long ago, I happened to be talking to a factory owner, when a flashily dressed young man rushed past his employer. As the young worker disappeared in his gleaming sportscar, the factory owner remarked:

"I wish I could afford his style."

To the casual listener, the statement might have been a reflection on the man's financial affairs. As a matter of fact, they were rather healthy. What he was referring to, of course, was the fact that as a successful capitalist, he simply could not "afford" to be seen as such. He should not be seen in anything less Low Key than an off-the-rack, ill-fitting, dull grey suit.

In short, in Europe when people dress poorly, they do so for one reason — poverty. In Australia, where one pays a great deal of attention to not being paid attention, poor dress is the aim.

First of all, when shopping for clothes, you must ascertain a poor fit. Features to look for are trousers that are slightly too short (as if they had shrunk on the buyer), of a material that crushes easily. Jackets must be a few years behind the fashion. Any fashion. If very narrow lapels are the vogue, then choose medium or wide. If wide lapels are the rage, choose medium or narrow. Real difficulties arise only when medium lapels come into fashion. As with all problematic choices in Australia, one suspects that the solution lies somewhere in alcohol.

Of footwear not more than two pairs are needed: brown shoes to go with blue, black or grey trousers, and black shoes to go with brown, fawn or white. The theme of this colour scheme should be carried right through the entire wardrobe.

In the "casual" footwear department, thongs can be worn with everything.

Dressing down for the occasion

The Australian woman has a lot more freedom because her choice of mis-matchable colours is so much broader.

The first stop of a woman shopping for clothes should be at the synthetics counter of a department store. This is where you will find the backbone of your summer or winter collection.

You need no more than six dresses, as Sundays may be spent in any brushed nylon brunch-coat. None of the dresses should be tainted by fashion or style. Go for the shirt-maker or cowl-neckline, as they always bunch up under a cardigan and look suitably gauche.

Blouses must be in a variety of prints so that they may be mis-matched in the highest number of permutations, while at the same time allowing you to look like everyone else.

Shoes and handbags need not be bought with any specific outfit in mind, as they can thus be grabbed at random from the pile at the bottom of the cupboard. The only requisite is that the shoes should at least match with . . . each other.

Why losers are heroes

When the English lose at competitive sports, the loss is attributed to bad luck. If an American loses, people blame inadequate training. When an Australian loses, no blame is attached at all. On the contrary, the event is regarded as a special achievement and the sportsman or sportswoman is praised for:

(a) trying very hard

(b) having given their all

(c) making 14th when they could have come last.

Besides glory and public recognition, the loser with enough failures to their credit also receives that highest accolade of all — becoming a universally recognised Little Aussie Battler. What gladiators were to the Romans, or kamikazes to the Japanese, Little Aussie Battlers are to the folks of the Fifth Continent. They are the legendary heroes and heroines who fight against all odds . . . and lose.

Spectators in a European or South American stadium will berate and curse their favourite team for the slightest mistake. Threatening the umpire with disembowelment is a must. Running onto the field with a machete is also quite popular. Declaring war on the rival team's country is a further variation.

One should not expect any of this in Australia.

While in other parts of the world a sports fan may come away from a lost match scarlet with rage, veins popping, only this side of a stroke, in Australia you must

"It's bronze, bronze, bronze for Australia! And the gold and silver went to — er, let me see . . ."

walk away from even the greatest disaster only ever so slightly sad. Calling your favourite bested player or team "great", "brave", "wonderful", or just plain "terrific" — humiliation after humiliation — is highly recommended. No compliment should ever be good enough.

A certain fascination for failure is a requisite of living in Australia. In simpler terms, while overseas people look forward to success, in Australia it is failure that's the source of greatest joy. If talking of friends, mention only those who lost all their money. If discussion touches on history, quote only lost battles, preferably by Australian or British troops. It's important to understand that whereas even kindergarten children can give you a list of battles lost by the "good guys" (Eureka, Gallipoli, etc.), most graduates find it hard to name a single battle where Australians have triumphed.

Australians have long accepted that there is something trustworthy about failure. Ned Kelly failed and he's revered for it. If only Howard Florey had just missed out on discovering penicillin — instead of actually discovering it — he could have had shopping centres named after him.

After all, if you win, nobody knows whether you're really doing your best. It might have simply been luck. If you come second, or third, or even last, people at least will know that you've exerted yourself. Then there is the added knowledge that if you've won, you've probably cheated, or tried too hard, at the expense of something in your personal life.

Whereas if you lose, at least you're honest.

The seven ages of man

I grew up with the traditional knowledge that man's life consisted of seven ages: infancy, childhood, adolescence, adulthood, middle age, old age and dotage. It came as a surprise, therefore, to find that in Australia the seven ages of man consist only of two: those under 25 and those past it.

Up to the age of 25, being an Australian involves a lot of hard work.

Men must sport an all-year-round suntan, wear zinc cream on their noses and maintain a general air of inhibited aggression. Women must keep up with fashions, brush their teeth four or five times a day, and find a place to go to every night irrespective of climatic (or climactic) conditions.

After 25 come the good times.

Now you can really let yourself go. This is a chance for the ladies to spend entire seasons in Target tentfrocks and Carmen heated rollers, perched on Keith Lord kitchen stools. For gentlemen it's an opportunity to let their stomachs hang over those tight King Gee shorts and play with their Taiwanese thongs while reminiscing with friends.

Everyone can relax now.

Most importantly, stay exclusively within your own age group. After two centuries of experimentation, Australians have found that knocking around only with one's contemporaries is the perfect way to age badly without ever really noticing it.

This way of all going down-the-hill together is Australia's answer to the secret of eternal youth.

Before 25

After 25

Feral Australians

Beyond the pages of your street directory and those easy to remember postcodes, live the feral Australians. Feral Australians live any place where they don't have government buses. They live on the edge of the feral frontier. They live in feral suburbs where the road becomes highwayish and video stores take on gigantic proportions.

Who are these people? Where do they come from? Transcending race, religion and geography, feral Australians inhabit vast tracts of semi-cultivated zones and are believed to have gone feral in the seventies when they were "settled in" to control an outbreak of waterslides and ten-pin bowling alleys.

Feral Australians can be sighted living close to huge shopping centres, near immense bottle shops and enormous hardware stores.

They look different.

Their acceptable currency are videos.

The females might wear stretch denims. The men could talk with hands in their pockets, shoulders hunched and their heads bobbing backwards and forwards. Everything they say ends with "and that."

"How are you going and that."

"I got seven b-grade movies for the price of one and that."

An Australian turning feral, spied escaping into a new development estate.

Never draw conclusions

Hiding in his Berlin bunker, Adolf Hitler saw that he was surrounded by Allied troops, concluded all was lost, declared the war closed and set fire to himself.

He wouldn't have done it had he been Australian. Australians, as a rule, are against drawing conclusions.

"Stone the crows! Bombs to the left, tanks to the right. Wonder if it's our boys. Maybe it's that other lot. Not much point worrying about it though. Reckon if I just keep mum a bit longer and stay down here in the bunker, things'll blow over."

Say you have moved into a small country town and it is your aim to integrate with the locals. Yours is the only CB radio in the street. Two days before Christmas, traditionally the stormiest time of the year, you hear on your set at 6.30 pm that flood waters have wiped out an entire area fifty kilometres to the north. It is your duty to tell everyone personally, then do nothing about it and turn up at the local pub for the rest of the evening.

But mere inactivity is no proof of your unwillingnes to draw conclusions. As a sign of your good faith, you should stand in the pub doorway as the waters rush towards you and express your bewilderment at the total suddenness of these things, and complain how December weather just isn't what it used to be.

There is constant pressure on the average Australian not to draw conclusions from events. You must show that you are straightforward, untainted by devious thought. You must be unable to predict anything more major than the third in the second at Randwick or Flemington on Wednesday.

"Relax, mate, it's only a summer shower."

Hence if it is likely that after the floods a cyclone will bear down, it would be most un-Australian to take any precautions other than tying up the dog.

Some time ago, I wrote a story about the experiences of a European doctor among Aboriginal tribes. One publisher perused my manuscript and shook his head.

"I am afraid this is not acceptable."

I looked sufficiently hurt to force an explanation.

"You predict here in your story that white Australians will be more and more willing to give back the Aborigines their rights as the Aborigines die out, no longer representing a danger due to their reduced numbers. I am afraid if we printed this, we'd be in hot water with everybody."

"It's how I view it."

"Oh come on, an Australian author's job is to describe things, not to add facts together and draw conclusions from them. It just isn't done. Where would that take contemporary literature? It's up to the readers, after all, to interpret it the way they want to."

Drawing conclusions, of course, is closely related to analysis. And analysis is another danger area that Australians don't get too close to.

A student — a young friend of mine who had recently arrived from Europe — achieved high marks in other subjects but failed her English exam. She took the offending essay back to her teacher, demanding an explanation for the low mark.

The teacher proved full of understanding.

"I've asked you here to analyse *Hamlet*. And so you go into long explanations of the characters' motives for their actions. And then you analyse Shakespeare's motives by pointing out his alternatives."

"Right. That's the way I learnt it in Europe", said the student.

"Well. In Australia, when you're asked to analyse a play like *Hamlet*, what we are really asking you to do is tell the story of *Hamlet*."

80

"Is that all? Why?"

"So we can be sure you've read the goddamn play!"

"But then why don't you just say 'describe *Hamlet*'?"

"Because 'describe' would mean 'give your opinion of it'!"

". . . The better known side of the family."

Never question ancestry

In some countries, every couple of years the Government issues a new textbook in which all past events have been thoroughly altered to suit the ruling government's immediate political needs. This not only helps the country's leader hang on to his job, but saves the trouble of having to interpret the present in terms of the past, as the past has obligingly adapted itself to suit the present.

By contrast, the history of Australia is a very simple affair. The truth can be neither altered nor denied. It is so widely known that a newcomer to this country need not even read the actual books. Just by talking to people, you can pick up all the historical background you need to know.

It is common knowledge, for instance, that the condemned convicts on that First Fleet were vastly outnumbered by the hundreds of officers sent over to guard them. This ratio discrepancy can easily be verified even now, two hundred years later, simply by talking to the huge number of families who can trace their lineage back to the officers of the First Fleet.

It is also commonly known that the country's early settlers, even if sent over as convicts, were generally guilty of crimes no worse than stealing a loaf of bread or a leg of ham, crimes which, owing to the harshness of the British judicial system of the times, were enough to have them most unfairly exiled to the Southern Hemisphere for life.

By a strange quirk of nature, those few convicts who *were* indeed guilty of heinous crimes and ended up on the shores of Botany Bay, proved to be either sterile or homosexual. This fortunate correspondence between criminality and incapacity to produce offspring was one of the future nation's lucky breaks. It saved countless generations from having to come to terms with any unpleasantness in their background.

Though there was a fair amount of interchange between early settlers and the local Aborigines, the relationship seems to have remained on a platonic level, with the two sides being more involved in deciding whether suburbs would bear English or native names, rather than in setting the common foundation of a new race of people. This is evidently why during the last two hundred years of Australian history, no prominent personality, political or artistic, has ever come forward and admitted to any Aboriginal ancestry — unless they were Aboriginal, of course.

Later another stroke of luck befell the future nation. Waves of young aristocrats descended upon the colony. Eccentric third and fourth sons of British earls and baronets, they came over for the sole purpose, it would seem, of sireing a host of middle-class families with double-barrelled names.

The descendants of these enthusiastic youngbloods are usually reticent beings who do not like to bring to light their elevated lineage. Instead they spend their time hiding from public glare (i.e. embarrassing questions) in clubs and associations designed to remind everyone of English upper class conditions of 150 years ago.

Don't be interesting

Before arriving in Australia, I thought of myself as an average conversationalist. It came as a shock to discover that, in fact, I was an "interesting" person.

On hearing my views and opinions, which to me sounded rather ordinary, Australians would look up with astonishment and mutter:

"That's *very* interesting."

"Really?"

"Mmmm."

One day I ran into another LCT (Little Confused Tourist), who described an almost identical bewilderment. Likewise, it had been bothering him for a while.

"Do you find me fascinating?" he began.

"Not particularly."

"Just as I thought. Yet I am always told by everyone that what I have to say is fascinating."

"What an amazing coincidence!" I exclaimed. "People are just as rivetted by my own conversation!"

We took a long hard look at one another. Could it be that we were smarter than either of us thought?

"It does look like it, doesn't it?"

It was only after some deep soul-searching and several litres of coffee that we arrived at the truth.

1 People in Australia are deemed
   "interesting" when what they have to say is
   of absolutely no interest to anyone.

2 The moment views, aspirations or beliefs
   are considered to be "fascinating", it is best
   to switch the conversation to the weather.

The high art of being dull

For some time now, it has been realised that the greatest bar to peaceful co-existence in Australia are people who have something concrete to say. Factual statements and detailed descriptions are simply too dangerous, and those who sport them should be contained, as they're likely to cause trouble.

In the spirit of the industrious nineteenth-century British who created in their country a complex system of locks, weirs and canals in order to stem the course of unruly rivers, Australians have diligently perfected various methods of diverting, re-routing and flattening ideas and facts, which if left unattended could upset the natural balance of things.

For this reason, though books and editorials may occasionally be factual and informative, face to face communication ought to be uneasy, vague and full of abstractions.

A Serious Conversation

"It's harder than ever to get anywhere these days."
"Not as hard as it used to be."
"Maybe it's just a matter of finding one's niche."
"I don't think that applies any more."
"Most people get the short end of the stick."
"There's lots to be said for working from nine to five."
"It's still a question of priorities."
"Not if you cared about what you were doing."

An Everyday Conversation

"Not bad, eh!"
"Could've been worse."

"My oath!"
"Makes you think!"
"You're not wrong there."
"Might change but."
"Pretty unlikely."
"You never know."
"Fair enough."

It's important to understand the principles that govern conversation in Australia. Not knowing them, you might make the mistake of trying to communicate.

In Australia you may say anything you wish, provided you do not back it up with facts. As most European-style conversation is too concrete and factual for Australian sensibilities, I take this opportunity to put forward some tried and true, evergreen conversational topics which are always likely to find favour with Australians.

1 Movies you missed on TV. Describe in meandering detail the circumstances that led you to come home late and catch only the last ten minutes of the movie under discussion. Lose interest once a person starts telling you the story.

2 Books. Never actually refer to books you've *read,* as that could lead to a difference of views. You're better off finding common ground with the other person by establishing what books both of you haven't read.

3 Winners you didn't back. This is an inexhaustible fount, as failure is a condition with which everyone can identify. Famous horses are the best. Lucky tips you've ignored just as good. In fact everything to do with horses except . . . winning.

4 Discussing or discovering common acquaintances could lead to serious blunders, so it's best to talk of people neither of you have ever met. Stars and politicians are

alright, but cookery experts are even better.

5 Talking of what you'd do if you won the lottery is very acceptable, since it permits both of you to rave on endlessly without having to listen to the other person.

6 Anybody can talk of the places they haven't been to as yet, but that promises to have no end in sight. It's best to talk of all the places you *wouldn't* want to visit. If you're from Sydney, mention Melbourne, or vice versa.

The National Etiquette

When unrestrained emotional Italians have a problem, they expect the whole world to take an interest, listen and help them solve it. Friends are selfishly contacted at two in the morning, hours are spent discussing the minutest details and litres of coffee and tears are poured out, while all manner of possible suggestions are put forward.

No Australian would stand for such behaviour.

In the United States, too, there are millions of brash, pushy and loud people running around with a variety of problems, complaining to family, friends, colleagues, psychiatrists, social counsellors, therapists, self-help organizations, positive thinking groups, or to anyone in subways and bars.

No Australian would stand for such behaviour either.

Australians are a polite and courteous people. Here it's considered bad manners to foist your problems onto others. You may be in the middle of a nervous breakdown, you may even have in-laws staying with you, but under no circumstances are you to admit to any difficulties.

"How's it going?"

"Great!"

"Are those your crutches?"

"Marvellous, aren't they?"

"What about the neck brace?"

"Brand new!"

While Australians have problems like everyone else, it is considered highly improper to voice these in intelligible exact terms. Polite Australians always talk about things that bother them with veiled cryptic comments. Well-bred people, they would never let on to what it is that's really wrong.

Under no condition are the issues that trouble you to be voiced in clear precise terms. Never actually refer to the problem itself. Always act as if your problem is something that's all over now and no longer of any consequence. Make it impossible for people to help you.

A German with matrimonial troubles, for example, will most likely take a swig of *schnapps,* turn to a friend and say: "I had an argument with Helga last night and she told me that if I didn't stop seeing other women and start coming home on time, she'd walk out on me."

This rude, obnoxious, over-precise way of talking about problems is simply not acceptable in Australia. An Australian in a similar predicament, after a long evening of inconsequential conversation with a friend, would remark:

"Jane's been strange lately."

"Oh, yeah?"

"She's been acting sort of funny."

"Hmmm."

"Makes one wonder . . ."

Another very important rule emerges here. Well-brought up friends in Australia know always to keep their distance and not get involved. The degree to which you can distance yourself from someone with a problem, in fact, and insist on not helping them solve it, is recognized as a measure of your good manners.

"It's up to you."

"I don't care either way."

"Whatever makes you happy."

Remember that should you, in a moment of weakness, take note of the problems of others or even offer to help them, there's a good chance that they'll shun you ever after for your tactless behaviour. You may know that the lives of Fiona, Gary or Greg are currently in a disastrous state but you must never say anything upon meeting. They may have lost their jobs or look like death warmed up, still you should simply overlook this and go along with a happy-go-lucky charade.

"You look great!"

"Thanks."

"Things must be going really well for you."

"Aha."

"It's good to see someone who's got it all together."

"Errr . . ."

On the other hand, should others ferret out that something *is* bothering you, should they get wind that you're in some kind of trouble, you ought to dismiss immediately whatever they say.

"Oh, no, I've already thought of that."

"I tried but it was no use."

"It's OK, it's all under control."

Unlike the rest of the world, the aim in Australia should always be to disguise your problem so completely that no one, preferably not even yourself, can understand any more the issues involved.

For this reason, it's best if problems in the family and in relationships, are simply left neglected. Do nothing about them. Ignore them until circumstances allow you only one possible solution:

"What else could I do?"

"There was no other way."

"It just sort of happened."

The key is to hold back from talking about the things that bother you until you've held back for so long that it has become absolutely impossible to talk about them anymore.

You are now ready to be a polite Australian.

"She just hasn't got her head screwed on right."

Australian Abstracts

What Pablo Picasso has done for portraiture, Australians have done for communication. They've turned a conventional approach to the relating of facts into an original modern form.

In the old traditional-style of story telling, practised say by Russians or Germans, people endeavour to relate something that's happened to them in a direct and exact manner.

Australians by contrast, see the ordinary relating of facts as unnecessary. For Australians it's the intrinsic subjective internalised point of view that is at the basis of the true art of antipodean communication.

Concrete	*Australian*
"What happened to your eye?"	"What happened to your eye?"
"It was ten minutes after midnight. I was putting on my pyjamas when there was a knock at the door. I opened up and two huge people burst in. The taller one, a man with a big red face, grabbed me by the arm and pushed me against the wall. His colleague, a fat woman with shiny steel teeth,	"It was unbelievable. It was incredible. I still can't get over the fact that things like this can go on here. I tell you we've got to do something. The authorities just have too much power in this country. I mean it was night time for god's sake! Actually when they arrived I thought it was a joke.

shoved a paper in my face.

" 'Is this flat 15?' she asked and ordered me to stand in the corner.

" 'No,' I said, 'It's 16. Have a look for yourself. There's a bit broken off the number.'

"The man goes out, has a look at the entrance, comes back without a word and gives me a black eye. As I closed the door, I heard them bashing down the entrance across the landing. My first thought was to warn them that 15 was really at the end of the corridor but then I decided to let number 17 cope with that."

No one's going to push me around like that and get away with it, let me tell you, no one! I would've told off the buggers then and there. Especially that awful woman who started to push me around. Honestly at first I thought she was a bloke.

" 'What do you think you're doing?' I demanded.

"I must have sounded really mad because suddenly they got cold feet and claimed they had made some sort of mistake. Mistake! How can you make a mistake like that? Galahs the whole lot of them!"

People in this country are keen to talk in an abstract way because they burn with a vital need to communicate the all-pervading, deeply underlying general mood of an event or situation.

"It was devastating. The hardest experience of my life."

"You might disagree but I think it could turn out to be good for the ego."

"I mean I thought I wouldn't live through it."

"You've got to be strong."

"All I could think was that I wanted to turn back the clock."

"I still think this is a situation with potential which is not to say that you shouldn't be prepared to go at least half-way."

"I suppose I've got to face reality even though I

probably missed out on a great opportunity to set everything right."

"You just went into it full pelt."

"It's traumatic but at least I feel I'm alive."

"Beautifully said."

Would you say the above refers to: a) a messy divorce? b) a big loss at the races? c) a face lift gone horribly wrong?

Never praise

A European wishing to praise someone, will throw his arms wide open, roll his eyes and declare in a loud voice: "You are undoubtedly the greatest, the most talented macaroni maker in Italy! You are not only a great craftsman but a gastronomical artist!"

Slightly exaggerated, to be sure, but on a continent of over five hundred million noisy souls, understandable. After all, how else is the message going to get through and make an impact? And then, perhaps the man *is* an artist, and why shouldn't he enjoy the appreciation of his craft?

In Australia, praise on such a lavish scale is not only unnecessary but positively dangerous. Australians would retort with comments like:

"What was all that about?"

"What's he *really* trying to say?"

"Is this a joke?"

"He must be drunk."

The Australian concept of praise runs in a different direction and as far away from absolutes as possible. In Australia, those wishing to show their appreciation will cautiously sum up the situation and then, after the necessary "errring" and "ummming", say in a quiet tone, something like:

"Not bad. Not bad, at all."

And if they *really* like it, they might even throw in a line such as "God, you must have been working hard" or, "I hope everyone appreciates the effort you put into this".

The aim is not only to avoid lavish praise but never to give unsolicited praise at all. In Australia, one may praise only if the other person has paved the way for it by rubbishing themselves first, with remarks like:

"I seem to have made a mess of things."

"I don't think I know what I am doing."

"It could have been better."

Of course, everyone understands that Australians, in running themselves down, are not really indulging in self-criticism but in fact giving the go-ahead to the other person for some medium-sized praise. The dialogue would run something like this:
"I don't know, this dress just doesn't fit me."
"Looks practically made for you."
"But I've chosen the wrong colour."
"I was about to say how well the colour suited you."
"It makes me appear too fat."
"You've never looked thinner."
"But I think I may have paid too much."
"No, no, you're so clever at finding bargains."
Take note. In the above type of situation, *not* praising could prove just as fatal as the offering at other times of unsolicited praise. For if you don't provide expected praise, Australians find themselves forced to take the last recourse and *praise themselves*.
"Hell, I don't know, I seem to have made a mess of things."
"Hmmm . . ."
"Even though I thought I was doing quite well."
"As a matter of fact . . ."
"Come on! It's not *that* bad!"
"I mean to say . . ."
"I happen to think that the whole thing is rather good, even if I say so myself."
"Errrr . . ."
"In fact, looking at it now, I would say it's excellent, bloody good, wonderful, terrific!"

"I'm so glad you like it!"

Never criticise

"This is the worst piece of execrable rubbish I've ever had the misfortune to come across. You are not only clumsy, stupid and worthless, but you have the effrontery to waste my time as well as that of the rest of Europe."

In Germany, you could be considered a fool, should you come up with anything less critical.

Don't try it in Australia.

In France, such a mild approach to the mistakes of others would not even rate a mention. The French, who take their critical faculties seriously, would closely examine the offending object. They are then likely to give a comprehensive list of those who have attempted it far more successfully but are still considered second-raters. This would follow with a list of all those who have done it well. It is highly likely they will then take the offending object, item, piece, etc., and throw it to the ground, spitting copiously, trampling it underfoot, and vowing to kill anyone who might ever again present them with such *merde*.

Don't try it in Australia.

In the United States, criticism is taken very seriously indeed. The American, who holds nothing more sacred than the concept of "progress", will come out with something like:

"Now look here, buddy boy, I don't care who and what you are, but you can't come up with stuff like this. What you'll really have to do is follow my advice, since I am much better, bigger, brighter and wiser than you!"

Don't try it in Australia.

When I first found myself in this country, I gained information about the place from movies, plays and television dramas. They displayed Australians as a forthright people who are forever involved in gutsy arguments, violent verbal skirmishes and fearless face-to-face confrontations; neither afraid to openly speak their minds nor resentful when others do so.

Nothing could be further from the truth.

Australians do not believe in the rights of others to be critical of their efforts at all. A Lucky Islander may be self-critical, true, but that is merely being Low Key, not unlike those Chinese Mandarins who used to refer to everything they owned or did as "humble".

This basic rule leapt at me the following way. An Australian friend, proud of his newly built outdoor barbecue, kept urging me for weeks on end to tell him what I thought of his handiwork. For weeks on end I assured him that it was very, very good. But no matter how much I insisted, he always closed the discussion with the remark: "Ah, it still needs a bit of work".

One day, as talk drifted onto the subject of his barbecue again, I decided to give in by agreeing with his own evaluation. So when he finally popped the question "What do you really think of it?", I told him, "Well, I imagine it stills needs a bit of work".

There was a painful and embarrassed silence. My friend simply sat there, and said nothing for a long, long time. After that I never heard from him again.

Criticism is the one thing Australians are simply not prepared for. They may request it. They may even tell you that they crave it. But you must never ever give in to the temptation. No matter how hard your friends, superiors or employees try to get an "honest" opinion out of you, no matter how earnestly you are assured that it is alright, that you can really speak your mind — don't soften. Don't give in. Hold to your initial opinion that everything is just perfect.

Say your friend has just brought around the plans for her new loungeroom, and she wants your honest thoughts on the subject.

You know better than to comment on how the chequered wallpaper clashes with the patterned carpet, or on the blue curtains with the salmon lounge-suite, or on the idea of having a glass coffee-table surrounded by fake rococco armchairs.

"It will look very nice", you remark enthusiastically.

But still she insists: "No, no, tell me the truth. If there is something you don't like, it can easily be changed".

(Hey, how do you change *everything*?)

"I tell you, it's wonderful what you've planned."

"But no, I want you to really tell me."

Finally you break down and say: "I think the Chinese rosewood sideboard doesn't quite fit in —"

"But can't you see?" exclaims your friend, outraged. "The pink in the wood will be reflected in the wallpaper! I've always decorated my own places. What's more, everyone's always been very positive! I really didn't expect you to be so small-minded. I'd never say something like that to you. Anyway, I worked for what I've got and I can do what I like. I have to leave now. I am going out."

In Australia, NEVER EVER CRITICISE. There are only two standard responses to criticism:

    1 They'll take years to forgive you, or

    2 You'll never hear from them again.

The problem with offering criticism in Australia lies in the fact that before you have finished speaking, people are ready with a levelling explanation of why things are the way they are — thus making whatever you say both irrelevant and insulting.

How to know more

An acquaintance tells you some information you have never heard or thought about before. Pick the correct reaction from the three given below:

> (a) "That's interesting."
>
> (b) "I didn't realise that."
>
> (c) "Tell me some more."

The correct answer is — none of the above.

The Australian reaction would be, of course:

"That can't be true."

This is the right response because you have limited life experience and you do not want anything or anyone to disturb it: you don't like conversations that stray too far away from accepted patterns.

And it shows that you know more than the other person anyway.

Grimacing for beginners

Try as you may to absorb local customs, imitate slang or penetrate Australia's national psyche, you will never be considered normal until you *look right* — until you look at ease in this unique environment. And what makes Australians *look right* are the faces they pull.

An honest Australian farmer who makes an impassioned speech on behalf of the country's struggling wheat growers, might just escape being labelled a "whinger". A mediocre actor in a corporate TV commercial, however, has only to jerk his neck and twitch the corner of his mouth and he'll be said to embody the indomitable fighting spirit of Australia.

Clearly, a grimace is worth a thousand words.

Here then are a variety of scowls, contortions and grins that you should learn to disport on various appropriate occasions:

Type one: "Uh-uh."

The most popular way to start really pulling faces is when somebody suddenly becomes passionate about a particular subject. This usually happens when you're in a group.

In Israel or Greece impassioned views would set the scene for an interesting discussion, but in Australia you and your friends must start to eye one another nervously, while frowning heavily with a series of painful

103

Keeping people at bay in public.

*"Oh-oh. Must be careful.
Someone over there likes me."*

The only way to get into the papers.

*"Uh-uh. They're getting
passionate about ideas."*

mouth contortions, to indicate a speaker who has gone off the rails.

If this doesn't work, re-form the party in such a way that the speaker is excluded. It's sure to achieve the desired results — as he is now talking to himself, while the rest of you telegraph to each other his obvious mental disturbance with a series of repetitive exaggerated grimaces.

Type two: "Oh-oh."

You've been invited to dinner. An attractive guest has started to gaze in your direction. Are you being asked to pass the salt? Is it someone next to you? Check. Eventually, you may have to accept the reality of the situation — someone is trying to flirt with you. What are you to do?

If you're a woman, compress neck, flare nostrils, tighten lips and show a congested expression. If you're a man, stiffen your face, look rigid and gaze intently just past the person who likes you. In France or Hungary, being admired makes people talkative and charming; in Australia if you're liked, wear a strict mask.

Type three: The Migraine Squint.

Here's a general grimace for when you're out and about.

The eyes are narrowed to accentuate the crows feet, the eyebrows are jammed into a straight line and the neck is locked into an angular position, allowing no sideward head-movement whatever.

Definitely to be worn in public places, this migraine-like-squint will give you the ability to walk down the street and not see anything, while warning people, at the same time to stay away from you.

Type four: Super-glue.

You're at a gathering. There's a rumour that someone

from a newspaper or a magazine has been spotted wandering with a camera among the crowd. It could be anybody. What can you do?

Start grinning.

Raise eyebrows to suggest naivete. Draw mouth-muscles right back. Bare teeth to the gums. Keep smile and eyes immobile as if they had been super-glued onto your face. Behave as in a trance.

In Australia, without the super-glue look they'll never print your photo in the papers.

Putting Australians at ease

Asians never really feel at ease until they've been allowed to talk about their family and background. Mediterranean people like to be touched on the arms or hands in order to feel at home with you. Assuring them that they are the most sensitive and sentimental beings you've ever met, will relax Slavonic people just nicely.

So what relaxes an Australian? What puts Australians most at ease?

For one, letting them stand by the front door, hand on the door handle, with the security of being able to leave whenever they wish. Suddenly, they will become very talkative. Of course, this is the time to extract that vital information you've been dying to find out all night.

When inside your home, do not insist on getting Australians to sit down. They're much more likely to stay longer if they can stand up, lean against a doorpost, or sit on the edge of a table. You'll see how much friendlier they are this way, how much more they'll trust you and take you into their confidence.

Be as friendly as you like on the phone, as Australians do like a good disembodied, impersonal conversation. But when meeting the same person face to face later, be sure to act really stitched up. In fact, you will achieve far more if you just turn away and pretend that you are still on the phone to each other.

An Australian at ease

A formula for making excuses

When apologetic Mediterranean acquaintances in Valencia, Salonika or Alexandria exclaim in their sincerest and loudest tones: "I know I swore and promised to be here at ten o'clock, however the reason I am three hours late is due to a most unhappy chain of events," you can be fairly certain that:

(a) the grandmother in question died ten years earlier;

(b) the douche-bag wasn't in the next apartment; and,

(c) the parrot never had a chance.

In Australia excuses are made in a very different spirit. Here such mundane and petty excuses would never pass muster. Excuses in Australia should either be on a grand scale or simply not made at all. Australians generally are mistrustful of those who do not get caught up in massive dramas and total disasters. This is a dramatic continent prone to spectacular catastrophes and your excuses, likewise, should reflect the violent and unpredictable nature of the environment.

"What happened?"

"I've been trying to get hold of someone at the dress shop but the woman was caught in a flash flood over the weekend and hasn't come back yet. I phoned the sales manager with the courier company but his father-in-law had just been struck by lightning. And the girl from the hotel I gave the money to has flown off to Cachexia in Brazil to look for her missing children."

"What about the theatre tickets?"

"Oh, my God! I must've lost them in the ambulance...!"

In many countries you are not expected to keep promises. In Australia, a country strong on Protestant ethics and Catholic conscience, you are. So how does one get out of them? How do you explain why the delivery cannot be made on time and in the quantities expected? "I've got a teeny problem with this item. There has been a bit of a production hiccup — the workers walked out on me and set fire to the factory, looters took most of the stuff and the police pinched the rest" — this might be a dandy excuse in Latin America but in Australia it makes a little too much sense. Go for the lateral approach.

"I couldn't possibly have fulfilled the order and I'm on the point of a nervous breakdown. My partner is threatening to go on holidays and I was incapacitated for three weeks. My secretary ran off with another boke and took the typewriter as well. I came back and there was all this dough missing from petty cash. The Cafe Bar broke down and now the rental company is threatening to repossess the answering machine."

Now observe a very simple rule emerges from all this. In Australia the more monstrous and unbelievable the excuse, the more likely it is to be taken as fact.

FOR THINGS THAT HAVEN'T BEEN DONE

"It's all ready, waiting for you."
"Great!"
"But I don't know where my assistant put it."
"I'll call back in an hour."
"Actually she's not coming back today."
"See you tomorrow then."
"The truth is I gave her the sack."
"So, how are you going to find it?"
"I might give the police a ring."
"The police?"
"She could have been carrying it when they fished out her body."

110

"I'm afraid I haven't had a chance yet."

"But you said Monday."

"Sorry, I've had a dreadful morning."

"Shall I ring back tomorrow?"

"As a matter of fact the other chap's gone off sick and I'm on my own here at the moment."

"At the end of the week perhaps?"

"Actually, we've had a lot of trouble with the computer."

"Next week then?"

"Well, that's when we're supposed to have the auditors in."

"How about a month from today?"

"We'll be moving premises then."

"What about December?"

"What about if *I* ring *you*?"

"When?"

"Let's make it next year just to be safe."

The aim of an excuse in Australia is to show people how much you respect them. The worthier they are, the more elaborate your story. Conversely, of course, you only tell the abrupt truth to those you hold in low esteem.

"Would you like a cup of coffee?"

The Great Australian Brain Drain

In other parts of the world it is understood that the human brain is capable of containing an unlimited amount of information and knowledge. But in Australia the brain is understood to be made of a highly strained and pressurised substance so that even by adding the slightest amount of information an overload can occur and cause the brain immediate collapse.

Hence you must understand that when people in Australia say: "I can't deal with that at the moment" or "I've got too much on my mind", "Come on, mate, I'm not Einstein", they are demonstrating to you the unique construction of the antipodean brain.

Australians are very selective about the information they put into their brains because they know that the brain is already full and taxed to the limit. After all you can't fit more than a pint of beer into a schooner.

For this reason you have to give plenty of notice so parts of the brain can be drained in order that new information may be fitted in. Hence when you ask Australians to do something, they invariably need time to do some draining.

This is evident in that complex exercise — inviting an Australian to do something on impulse.

"Would you like to sit down?"

There is a pause.

"Er, thanks, no . . . I don't think I can . . . Er . . . Um . . . I really should be going . . . I don't think . . . I'm a bit of an aah .. . . Er . . ."

What is happening here?

The face manifests a startled look as if they're slightly indignant. This is not the case. They are in the initial stages of draining.

AUSSIE BRAIN: Oh, this person just asked me to sit down . . . What do they mean? . . . (*Impossible to understand at this stage because brain is already full*) Am I being ordered around? . . . Am I being exploited? . . . Why should I have to sit down? . . . (*Brain starts draining process*) Oh, that's right, I am a guest . . . (*Minimum amount of space being created*) I better sit down then . . . (*Accidental reversal of the process, brain stops draining.*) But not just yet because I am not ready to do that yet . . . And I don't want this person to think I'm easy or that I can be pushed around . . . (*Brain starts emptying once again*) I suppose I could sit down now but I don't think there's any particular hurry is there? . . .

To sum up:
1. Australians always have to stop doing something in order to do something else, meaning the brain is full.
2. Resentment is the first reaction. They'll have to drain the brain a bit.
3. Relief comes when they realise that the brain is empty.

The best hours of business

COMPARED to other nations Australia is a free and informal country where business is transacted virtually at any time and under any conditions. I realised this when making my first tentative enquiries regarding the best hours for getting in touch with people.

"Take my advice," said a friend. "You can contact people in Australia any time you wish but just don't ring today."

"Why not?"

"It's Monday morning."

I was intrigued. "What happens Monday mornings?"

"Everyone is too busy telling each other about their weekend."

Grateful for the tip, I promised to heed my friend's suggestion. Since then I have found, however, that for maximum efficiency the following times, apart from Monday mornings, are also not particularly good for business:

Monday afternoons:	Because the pleasure of talking about the weekend has worn off and people are suffering from the shock of returning to work after a break. Everyone is grumpy.
Tuesday mornings:	Because it's when you do Monday's work.
Tuesday afternoons:	The first chance everyone's had to catch up with the boss.

115

Wednesday mornings:	You're on top of the crest looking down at the next distant weekend. Everyone has to go to the pub or out shopping to buck up their spirits.
Wednesday afternoons:	Catching up with work you should have done on Wednesday morning.
Thursday mornings:	Takes all morning to get your pay.
Thursday afternoons:	Since it's payday everyone will stay a little longer at the pub. Afterwards they'll be in a good mood, true, but too good to transact any business.
Friday mornings:	Everyone is too busy planning the weekend.
Friday afternoons:	Usually people take all-afternoon lunches or else return to work soused.

My mention of Saturday mornings and Sunday as possible dates for transacting business met with a terrible derisory laughter from almost everyone.
"You've got to be joking! It's the weekend!"

The perfect job

ASK a contented Norwegian about his particular occupation and he would most likely tell you the precise size of the trawler he works on, the type of seasonal fish he and his six colleagues catch, the amount they haul in, the kind of nets they employ and the specific tasks he is expected to perform.

Ask a dedicated Swiss about her job and she will answer you with the particulars of the bank that employs her, what her position is, where she stands in the company hierarchy, what her exact duties are, how long she's been employed and how many years before she expects to receive a promotion.

Satisfaction and personal success in Australia are measured in completely different terms. After all, while the rest of the world was still groaning under the yoke of post-war reconstruction, Australians were already enjoying the world's shortest working hours.

For this reason in Australia it's not the actual job a person holds but the time off from it that indicates a person's status. You can recognize successful Australians by the way in which they discuss their careers.

"I've got a great job."

"Oh yeah?"

"I don't have to start work till ten in the morning."

"Well, I'm usually off by five to four."

"But we get every third Friday off."

"We get three days off before we need a medical certificate."

"We get automatic compo for five days."

"I get two bonus flexie days a year."

"I get seasonal bonuses AND tea money."

"Our strikes are fully subsidised."

"My redundancy payments include six months of unused canteen allowance."

"My termination payout gives me one work-free year."

Other topics that may be brought up successfully in conversation are long service leave, study leave, birthing class leave, maternity leave, paternity leave, holiday leave loading, superannuation, housing subsidies, low interest company loans and the free use of a car on weekends.

With a little adroitness you can avoid all mention of what either of you actually does for a living.

Easy ways to put things off

THE distinctive principle that governs decision-making on the Fifth Continent must be studied by all those who wish to reach any real success here, and understood by those who wish to have insight into the secret life of the nation.

When the Vietnamese need to make a decision to do something, they panic a little, deliberate a little and then carry out the task promptly and without regrets. The French will make a decision almost instantaneously because they don't want anything to interfere with their love-life or gastronomical pleasures. Americans make decisions promptly because they live in mortal fear of missing out on profits.

Practised Australians, on the other hand, know that the best method to cope with decision-making is to put things off for as long as possible. After all, this way you are not going to make any mistakes.

"Must have you over at our place sometime."

"I can do the essay the night before it's due."

Uniquely Australian, the urge to delay, defer and not decide to act just yet is as much part of the nation's heartbeat as a six-stroke Holden engine.

"Let's all have a good think about it first."

"Should get together one day and talk things out."

"Can I phone you back?"

All great nations pulsate to an inner cadence which regulates the rhythm of their lives and destinies. To randy Brazilians this pulse is defined by the orgiastic beat of the *samba*; to melancholy Portuguese by the despondent measure of the *fado*; to quixotic Poles dreaming of independence for four hundred years by the frenzied pace of the *mazurka*.

Australia's secret inner rhythm is defined by the beer commercial. The principle behind the beer commercial decrees that no matter how great their level of activity, speed, bustle, animation, briskness, vigour, push, drive, pep or energy, what Australians really aspire to is inertia.

You must learn, therefore, to pace yourself. Putting things off must become as second nature to you as sleeping is to wombats. The idea is to deliberately rhythmically delay, postpone and put off taking action until the whole decision making effort grinds to a halt.

Like a classical tragedy this process has five distinct acts or stages:

1. It's important to slow things down right from the start. When the garbage piles up, suggest squashing beer cans really flat so you only have to throw the garbage out once a week. When rain pours in through the roof, resort to blocking holes with shopping bags. "Plastic is probably even more resilient than tiles." Accompany all proposals with little self-congratulatory remarks to convince everyone that everything's under control:

"Hey, why didn't I think of it before?"

"The answer was there before our eyes!"

"We're really lucky that I've come up with this idea."

2. Slow things down further by looking for lateral solutions. In other words solutions that require more talking than doing. "There's no point in halting sewerage flowing onto the beach unless we can work out how to stop the process once and for all."

Convince yourself and others that the task isn't urgent. Nip it in the bud.

"Surely we have more important things to do than fret about a few cancelled orders?"

"All places this size have damp troubles in winter."

"I don't think a meeting is going to mend these broken pipes."

"It's only temporary soil erosion."

If people panic about a crack in the bloc wall make it clear that there's no urgency whatsoever. "They've been predicting the fall of the tower of Pisa for eight hundred years."

3. Put off the decision to take action for an indeterminate time, because of insurmountable difficulties. "I don't care how urgent it is, I just don't think we should oppose tree-felling around here unless we're going to come up with a substitute for paper."

Warn everyone of the immensity of the obstacles involved. "There's no point in covering the hole in the roof with new tiles unless they're going to match the old ones and they haven't made these type of tiles since Menzies was Prime Minister."

Demonstrate the wastefulness of trying to cope with something you have no control over. "What's the point of making a firebreak around the house when just one flying spark is enough to set it alight?"

If people are still not swayed, take the total disaster approach. "All right, we do make the corruption public, but what's to guarantee that the whole police force is not going to crumble like a pack of Weet-Bix?"

4. Place the blame for not taking a decision squarely on the shoulders of others. "Sure we should do something about these pot holes but how can we given existing council regulations?"

Spread the responsibility around. "The whole place from the front room to the dunny is in danger of collapse but nobody seems to care!"

Make it general. "If it was just our products that were returned I would say let's do something about it, but it's the whole footwear industry."

Explain that the infestation is a widespread condition and whether the individual does or doesn't do anything about it is not going to make one iota of difference. "In the Middle Ages there was nothing at all anyone could do until the brown rats arrived and wiped out the black ones."

5. Total abandon. "I can't be bothered with my kids anymore."

Grind the need for decisions to a complete halt. "Trying to make a decision about the shipping yards was a waste of time from the first."

Make everyone accept that there is nothing to be done. "Let's face it, we couldn't have helped, welfare agencies just reach their natural end just like people."

Emphasise that even if something could have been done, it's simply too late. "It looks like the Department of Main Roads will be reclaiming the whole housing estate after all."

Everyone is happy and relieved now.

"We agreed it was in everybody's interest to do nothing."

"The truth is we simply weren't ready to make a decision."

"I don't know what came over us to even consider it."

Easy ways to say get lost

THE Chinese are always careful to point out that theirs is the subtlest language in the world, wherein each word may be spoken in four different tones that correspond to four different and distinct meanings. Australians, with a country the size of continental China, are no less sophisticated in their use of language.

As a case in point take the word "mate".

The Standard Oxford Dictionary attributes no less than seven different meanings to the word "mate", all clearly distinct from each other. Undeterred by this Australians have proceeded to generate a further series of interpretations. The result has given birth to a great deal of misunderstanding.

Many overseas people erroneously believe "mate" to be merely an expression of friendliness and, wishing to please Australians, employ it on all possible occasions as a signifier of their good intentions — much to the amusement of locals who, having been brought up with all the shrewd uses of the word, understand intimately its Byzantine gradations.

Here is a brief sample of the variety of local connotations:

All right, mate	Forget it
Coming, mate?	I'd rather go on my own
Good to see you, mate	What the hell are you doing here?
Good day, mate	Make it quick
How are you, mate?	You're nobody important
I'm telling you, mate	I'm lying through my back teeth

Geez, mate	How stupid can you get?
Listen, mate	You won't understand anyway
What you reckon, mate?	You better agree with me on this or else
Hang on, mate!	Shut up or I'll bash your face in!

So if you wish to get rid of someone as they appear in the doorway of your workshop, office, home, room, it's easy to make them uncomfortable:

(a) open the door wide

(b) look them straight in the eye

(c) using a broad sweeping gesture usher them in with a cheery "Come in, mate!"

Any sensitive well-behaved Australian will know immediately that what you really mean to say is "I wish you would get lost."

"I reckon if I don't greet anybody in the lift, ignore the guys in my section, avoid talking to the tea lady, and just grunt in the canteen, I should have enough energy to go socialising tonight."

Energy conservation

Saving your energy is part of the national conscious-ness of a country that until a few years ago had very little environmental awareness. Australians may not know it, but they have become world leaders in the field.

To give an example, in a wasteful country like America if a person sights someone he knows he will start waving his arms, uttering any number of loud noises and expending a great deal of vitality in greeting this friend.

An Australian even at the peak of physical condition is wary of such extravagance.

The most energy conscious will try to avoid the gaze of an acquaintance, or even of a friend, well in advance. Making your way down corridors where you are likely to meet colleagues, walk with your eyes planted to the ground. As soon as you enter a lift stare only at the panel of buttons. At home, make sure your gaze does not stray from the T.V. or newspaper onto your children.

After all there is only a limited amount of energy to go around and one never knows when one might need it.

How to make a cup of tea

For generations, the Japanese have been allowed to get away with the notion that theirs is the most advanced tea-making ceremony in the world. While no one disputes Japanese sophistication, it must be pointed out that the improvements wrought by Australians to the tea-making process have put this country in the forefront of the world's traditionalists.

Essential to the Australian tea ceremony is the concept of time. The Australian tea maker's aim is to put off the actual completion and serving of tea-proper for as long as possible.*

For this purpose, the Australian tea ritual begins long after the arrival of guests — especially if the guests were unexpected. In fact, its precise starting moment comes when the host begins to make vicious eyes at his wife, in response to which she reluctantly asks if anyone is thirsty.

"Tea would be nice", the parched guests mumble with swollen tongues.

Having finished her cigarette, the hostess jumps up, exclaims "Tea it is then!" and disappears into the kitchen, where she lights another cigarette.

After wiping down the sink, she fills the kettle to the very top with water, and re-emerges into the loungeroom, where she interrupts everybody by saying, "Water's on".

There's a stunned silence. The hostess puffs with

*Thereby, symbolically at least, delaying the twin processes of death and credit card repayments.

deep satisfaction, casting her husband murderous glances. (Legs on the coffee table, he reclines in complete immobility.) After the screeching of the kettle, she stubs out her cigarette and departs once more.

She looks for the sugar jar and picks out the hardened bits. She then puts some tea-leaves into the tea-pot but decides that tea-bags would be easier, so empties the unused tea-leaves into the sink.

Grabbing the carton of milk from the fridge, she carries it with the sugar bowl into the loungeroom, where she says, interrupting again, "Won't be long".

Back in the kitchen, she tries to match four cups and saucers, which she then transports into the loungeroom, saying, "Oh, I forgot the spoons".

Tea is now almost ready to be served. It is just that the water has to be re-boiled, as twenty minutes have elapsed since she switched off the kettle.

Keeping an eye on the water, she lights another cigarette. "Be with you in a sec!" she calls out to her guests as she finally pours the boiling water into the tea-pot.

Her entrance is greeted with gasps of delight.

"Ah, I'm looking forward to this!" says one.

"Nothing like a quick cuppa", says the other, without any irony at all.

Pleased, the hostess invites everyone to help themselves to tea, remarking with another murderous glance at the husband who still hasn't moved an inch:

"Sorry we don't have any biscuits, but Bruce ate them all last night."

The secret of service

SAY the word "service" to Italians and they will probably visualise a waiter with six plates of food piled on each arm racing between rows of noisy customers. Service to most Chinese means a seven-course meal prepared by the time they have taken their places at a table set for twelve. To Americans, service means a twenty-five storey hotel rising out of the Kalahari Desert that offers customers ten different varieties of freshly made hamburgers at three in the morning.

Say "service" to Australians and most will think of:

(a) John Newcombe in a Wimbledon final
(b) a grease and oil-change for the family car
(c) the Armed Forces, or
(d) a long and tedious church wedding.

Australians, on the whole, are a rugged and spartan race and do not associate the concept of service with the comforts of life.

In Australia service is perceived in a very different light.

"I hate to disturb you and I know it's 12.30 and probably your lunch-break but do you think I could possibly have a look at the menu?"

For service from trades people you are well-advised to consult a reputable astrologer or numerologist to see if they will manage to turn up. Certainly booking their time, telling them it's urgent or offering more money as you would in other countries doesn't work.

Being so democratically-minded Australians do not think that one of two people with equal rights before nature and the law ought to engage of their own free will in something as humbling as service.

"Waiter!"

It's a good idea to crawl for service.

First you try to get through on the phone three or four times. Finally a voice answers. "Ah yes! I'll get someone else who knows all about spare parts."

You hang on for five minutes. A new person picks up the phone.

"Yes?"

You make your request all over again.

"Wait while I see. I'll have a look."

Ten minutes later:

"Did you say it was an '80 or an '85 model?"

"'87."

"Wait a minute."

Shuffle of feet as the person goes off to inspect the stock again. More slow shuffling as the person comes back and picks up the phone.

"There's only an '84 model. I'll have to check when they changed the design."

After another interval you find out they do have the right piece after all. It's agreed that the item will be put aside and you will pick it up as soon as possible.

You get there. It's not waiting for you.

"Excuse me."

"Hang on. I'm serving someone."

"But there's no one here."

"They've gone to the car to check on a part."

Rule One: Never let people sense that you want something in a hurry. Should Australians get the scent that you're desperate for something, in a hurry or at all keen then things will slow down to a crawl.

Fifteen to twenty minutes later it's your turn.

"There's no more parts. We're out."

"But someone told me they put one aside for me."

"Don't know anything about that."

"I was told it'll be on the counter."

"Not here."

You may insist as much as you like but no one is willing to search for anything. Finally an employee turns up whose voice is strangely familiar. Hope springs eternal.

133

"I am the person who phoned you earlier... Have you the part?"

"Yeah. Yeah. Just let me get organised."

Rule Two: Because Australians are a proud and independent people it's best to give an order then quickly turn aside so that they have a chance to carry out your request without feeling servile.

Some considerable time later the employee comes back and tackles the indifferent colleague.

"Where's that thing?"

"What?"

"Where did you put that part I put over here?"

"What part?"

The fight lasts anything up to ten minutes.

"What are you talking about?"

"I had it wrapped in a piece of paper."

"Oh that! It's over there. I thought it was your lunch."

Now to the price.

"I'll have to look it up."

Following a hefty wait a figure is finally established.

"There's also sales tax."

"How much?"

"Let me check."

Another wait.

"What's holding it up now?"

"We're changing over to computers."

Docket in hand at long last, you go over to the cashier.

"Geez," says the cashier, "you're lucky. We're just about to close."

Curbing your generosity

Everyone (in Europe, that is) knows that it is easier to be generous than mean. In generosity, one gives and forgets about it. Meanness, on the other hand, takes forethought, planning, organisation and a good deal of dodging.

Yet for all its straightforwardness, generosity in Australia is fraught with many dangers. A European friend of mine found this out after buying flowers, chocolates and other unimportant gifts for his Australian mates.

"You won't believe this", he exclaimed in agitation on one particular occasion, "but we went out last night, four of us blokes from the office, and we stayed out till past midnight. It was pleasant — everyone was nicely tense and unspontaneous — and we all enjoyed ourselves saying things we didn't mean and purely for effect, when right at the end I went and did a stupid thing."

"Don't tell me. You drank too much!"

"I probably didn't drink enough. One minute we were sitting around, punching each other on the shoulders, the next moment I was at the bar settling the whole account."

"Good God! You didn't!"

"I know! How the hell will I face my friends now? There will be this terribly embarrassing gulf between us, especially in lifts and at the staff canteen. They'll never invite me out in case I do it again."

"Well, would you like to go out with them again?"

"Yes, I would like to make sure that there are other such occasions. I won't do anything foolish. As it is, half the office refuses to talk to me because I've given them

When professional help is needed to curb your generosity

small gifts on the odd occasion."

"So why do you do it?"

"I don't know. They're only inexpensive items, bu
seems to be enough to send people scampering do
passageways and back into the lavatory when they :
me coming."

"You've turned into the office creep!"

"Isn't it terrible? I'll have to seek professional help.'

After extensive treatment, he was, he said one d
finally "cured".

"No more digging into my pockets before everyc
else", he said with pride. "No more sneaking behi
people's backs to settle restaurant accounts. Now I s|
the bill down to the last cent, and keep an eye out
whose turn it is to shout at the pub. I can even visit
friends without taking any presents, and if talk comes
money, I've learnt to change the topic quick smart
case anyone asks to borrow some."

"And are you happy?" I asked him.

"Very. But there is one problem. Now it's my
European friends who avoid me."

The dinner party

To be invited for dinner to a middle class Australian home is quite an honour. It is also a good idea to eat a decent meal beforehand.

The basic idea behind an Australian dinner party is to get together a group of men and women who are all used to eating at 6 pm, and then not feed them till well past nine.

To be fair, some bridging alimentation *is* provided about an hour after your arrival, in the shape of "savoury snacks". Make sure you are standing near the kitchen door as they are brought out, since the life span of these snacks, like those of invisible atomic particles created in laboratories, can only be measured in nanoseconds.

Before the actual dinner, you are expected to drink and join in the mixed conversation. "Mixed", of course, does not mean women with men. It's the topics and the drinks that are mixed. Clarice Thong, Duchess of Highborough, in her "Souvenirs Of An English Parasite's Wife", wrote of her visit to Australia in the early 1970s:

> There is something terribly quaint about a country where men stand at one end of a room and women at the other. It's a very sensible way to behave given their condition, and Hewlett and I often wondered why it had not been made compulsory behaviour in other Third World countries as well.

If forced into the position of having to make conversation with women, Australian males are usually careful not to say anything definite or concrete that might inadvertently reveal some secrets about themselves or their feelings. They prefer, instead, to gesticulate a great deal in graphic depiction of the "form" of things, rather than their "content". It is also customary to accompany all this arm-waving with a nervous laugh, in order to reassure "the ladies" that what is being said is not in the least important.

Australian females, on the other hand, prefer to take the stance of one left in charge of a large heap of rights and wrongs that desperately need sorting.

For this it's best to screw up your eyes and look slightly indisposed. Firmly clenched hands and a rigidly held body also help emphasise a point. The general aim is to stop the male in his tracks.

Lines of dialogue to be used for this purpose can be as follows:

"Oh, I don't think anyone would agree with that."

"How can you make such a statement!"

"You're being grossly unfair."

"That's a terrible generalisation."

After a few such exchanges, dinner may be served.

In China, a country with a three-thousand-year culinary history, dinner that does not consist of at least seven to ten dishes, is considered ill-mannered indeed. And this in times of famine. In Germany, home of the Large Portion, a plate that does not groan under vast quantities of food is simply not worth looking at.

By contrast, the Australian hostess, in her endeavour to be sophisticated, will spend a great deal of energy making sure that she has counted the right numbers of everything. You know, six guests — six t-bone steaks, six potatoes and three halved grilled tomatoes. After all, there is nothing better than simple, wholesome food.

"I'm sorry but someone here must have helped themselves to an extra potato."

"Oh, it must have been me."

"I'm afraid I'll have to ask for it back. Otherwise John misses out."

"John may have my portion too if he wishes."

"No, no, I want you to tell me what you think of it. I feel I may have overcooked it a bit."

Everybody knows that this is a trap. The Australian hostess, mother, wife, aunt or hotel proprietor just loves to run down her own cooking, to a point where it is downright difficult not to agree with her.

But, of course, you must never do this.

"I am sorry the cake's so dry."

"It's beautiful."

"I think I made it a bit too sweet."

"No! No! I love it!"

"I used all the right ingredients but added too much lemon."

"I can hardly taste it."

"But it's a lemon cake!"

"Oh."

"So you don't like it!"

No matter how cleverly you might be baited, hold steadfast to a contrary opinion. Whatever it is. Even if the food is tough as plastic, or drier than the mouths of Burke and Wills in the desert, you must insist that whatever you're eating is just perfect.

"Mmmmmm. That spoonful of gravy was superb."

"Thank you. I didn't make too much because I didn't want anyone to have to drown the natural taste of the meat."

"Ah, the meat! I've even eaten the grissle off the bone."

Just remember that you are expected to talk about the food. Endlessly. Australian guests know by instinct to praise everything placed before them, whether they like it or not. Having been trained at home over mother's cooking, they show their appreciation for every morsel they get.

The party

Since Australia represents a new society, new social laws apply. In the Olde Worlde style party, the rules of etiquette were set down rigidly. In the New World style party, there are no rules whatsoever. Everyone is free and spontaneous. However, several customs have inevitably developed over the years, and they are worth mentioning.

1 If you throw a party, under no circumstances are you to introduce guests to each other. The idea is to let people wander round aimlessly, feeling left out.

2 You must never have enough food to go round.

3 If you're a guest, and you brought along a bottle of scotch or champagne, make sure you point out to everyone what a fine label it is, but do not share it with anybody.

4 Ascertain that the house is furnished with wall to wall shag, then ash your cigarette on the carpet. On the other hand, if the party happens to be held outdoors, be careful to ash into someone's half-empty beer can.

5 Do not go around trying to express ideas or have an intelligent conversation. If you do end up in a huddle with someone, be careful

141

to talk only of things you know nothing about.*

6 Never invite an equal number of men and women. The aim is to keep up an artificial shortage so that after midnight, the boys can end up dancing with the boys.

7 Make sure that you leave the party so drunk that you can't remember where you parked the car. Walk about the suburbs till dawn, singing songs from beer commercials.

There are several topics that must never be mentioned at parties: real feelings, true beliefs, actual voting habits, personal habits, any habits, history of mental illness, your income, your parents' income, the other person's income, and anything not in the the papers or on TV.

How to motivate an Australian

THE surest way to motivate people in Australia to accomplish anything is to make them feel that whatever it is they are attempting to perform, it is something they couldn't possibly do.

This is your cornerstone of success in Australia. In the United States you exhort the inhabitants with declarations such as: "For America, the flag and an Adidas commercial!" In France the best encouragement is a medal. In Iran you promise martyrdom. But in Australia you motivate people by telling them things such as:

"You haven't got a hope in hell."

"It's a lost cause."

"You'll never make it."

Should you wish to spur on a lagging sportsperson in China, you would exclaim, "For the Party and a bicycle all of your own!" In Australia, however, you would simply utter: "Not on your life!" or "I reckon you've got less than one chance in a million," or "There's just no way you can do it."

These key words have the miraculous effect of transforming the average person from Coolangatta or Tallandoon into a high achiever. Words which might bring to a halt the overly touchy Spaniard, send into decline the hypersensitive Mongol or make the thin-skinned Indonesian lose all hope, ignite your basic Boggabrite into unrestrained action with the same impetus as a powerful anabolic steroid, and they set about achieving their goals.

143

"What? I'll show them!"

"Just give me half a chance!"

"It makes my blood boil!"

You must understand clearly that words of traditional positive thinking have the reverse effect.

Saying "I reckon if anyone can pull it off, mate, you can," results in the person giving up after six months.

Saying "Australia's best chance for gold," results in the athlete coming fourth.

Saying "You'll knock the spots off them!" results in the pop group returning from their tour by cargo ship.

But say "You're just tilting at windmills," "Not on your Nelly!" or "You couldn't knock the skin off a rice pudding," and it becomes a different matter.

The secret is that if you put pressure and responsibility on the shoulders of Australians they panic or go to pieces. Expressions such as: "You'll kill 'em!" and "It's in the bag" and "Hot favourite" have the opposite of the desired effect by applying the constraint of having to perform. But take away the urgency and the obligation and your Australians blossom like an orange tree without a black plastic bag over it.

"I think you've shot your bolt."

"You've as much chance as a fart in a windstorm."

Suddenly they feel uplifted, responsibility is taken off their shoulders, and they experience a primeval energy release in their minds and bodies.

"Who do you think you are?"

"I'm going to teach them a lesson they'll never forget!"

Hell hath no fury like an Australian scorned.

"No hope . . .! Give it in . . .! No chance . . .! Doomed to fail . . .! No way you can do it . . .! Save yourself the embarrassment . . .! Pathetic . . .!"

Mother's Day

March the 8th throughout the world is "Women's Day". On this date, all men from young to old, give flowers, gifts and special dinners to the females in their lives, in appreciation of feminine attributes and achievements. On Women's Day the entire female sex is celebrated.

Such a manifestation of feeling has been found to be insufficient in this country. While every Australian's mother is undoubtedly a female, lumping her together with the rest of the world simply did not seem fair, seeing that her roles and responsibilities are so much greater.

To begin with, Australian mothers allow their children a vast deal of freedom and youngsters grow up with hardly any restraints. It is rare to see limitations imposed even upon the youngest of infants. Children are permitted to develop naturally and unencumbered from birth, according to the best pioneering traditions. There *are*, however, a few limitations which even the most liberal-minded mother must observe, if her offspring are to fit into this society.

1. All curiosity manifested by children for objects or ideas, ought to be countered and rebuked with a healthy:

"Don't you touch anything!"

"Don't be a sticky beak!"

"It's none of your business!"

Should any adult relative or friend address your children directly, a mother must always make a point of jumping in and answering for the kids:

"Bianca doesn't know."

"Trent is too young to understand."

"Jane is not feeling well today."

Embarrassing displays of affection on the part of the children for other people, ought to be prevented at all costs with a stern:

"Don't bother Uncle Bill!"

"Leave Aunty Violet alone!"

"Stop being a nuisance!"

2. Overseas mothers waste a lot of their children's time with pointless reminiscences, idle dreams, silly pranks and foolish romantic stories. Australia must be the only country in the world where a mother's conversation is entirely instructional, as she is determined to improve her children at every chance she gets.

"Tidy your room."

"Hang up your clothes."

"Rinse your plate."

3. Only Australian mothers know how hard it is to teach kids the meaning of patience. Techniques differ from household to household, but making children wait for their nourishment is perhaps still the most effective.

The instant a child asks to be fed or arrives home hungry and expecting alimentation, it is a mother's duty to reply with a clear:

"Wait a minute!"

"I'm busy!"

"I've only got one pair of hands."

It's advisable to keep the kids waiting for anything from twenty minutes to an entire afternoon. You certainly shouldn't just dish out the food as youngsters might start taking it for granted. The advantage is that it prepares them for life in Australia, where things always take a little longer than everyone thinks.

In recognition of these and many other admirable attributes, Australians have set aside the second Sunday in each May to celebrate with a great deal of devotion mothers right across the country.

On this day from early morning everyone in the family is busy preparing for the festivities. The men fight over who'll make the toast, the girls bring flowers and chocolates. Older children make an effort to turn up. They might take you out for a meal, or just give you nylon brunchcoats, cordless irons, fluffy pink slippers, tools to turn carrots into flowers, or maybe even a non-stick skillet.

Bringing down children

Some countries, like Italy and France, hold to the belief that children can be *born* with special talents or aptitudes. In Russia and Japan it is believed that children *trained* from a tender age will show marvellous abilities. Australians, imbued as they are with the spirit of fairness, hold both these views to be untrue. In Australia, it is believed that not only are children all born the same, but that they must also be actively discouraged from becoming in any way different, more capable or better than their peers.

While overseas the aim is to bring children up, in Australia the idea is to bring them down.

The process has a few basic steps.

1 Childhood ought to consist of a series of "don'ts", uttered clearly and with dramatic authority from early infancy*. Under ideal conditions, "don't" should be the very first word a baby hears. The purpose is to impart on the child a vague feeling of guilt for every one of its actions, by never explaining what it is that's wrong.

2 If children show a natural passion for playing the piano, writing poems or leaping over tall fences, it's important to force them to spend as much time and

* *It's actually the middle classes who say "don't" to children. The upper classes prefer to say "do", i.e.:*
  • *Don't bother me! (middle class)*
  • *Do sit still! (upper class)*
  • *Don't touch anything on the shelves! (middle class)*
  • *Do help mummy with the shopping! (shopping class)*

"He's never gonna play for Australia."

energy as possible away from the things they're good at or have a talent for, in the hope that they'll lose interest or become too discouraged to go on.

"What are you up to?"
"Practising."
"What, again?"
"I'm sorry."
"You'd be better off doing something else."

Should they persist in doing things they're talented at, keep pointing out all the difficulties that lie ahead. Advise them to get involved with backyard cricket, pinball machines or the local pool instead. Explain that by being good just at the one thing will make them boring and unpopular with friends.

3 No one quite understands why some Australian children are born with a competitive spirit. Often terribly normal families bring forth kids who want to succeed in life for no explainable reason. Baffled parents have been urging the Government to study the problem for years. The affliction strikes at random and blights the unlikeliest youngsters. You may care to try the following popular remedies:
   (a) Don't put any energy into developing the children;
   (b) Keep them in a learn-free cocoon for as long as possible;
   (c) Make certain they grow up no better than yourself — the motto here ought to be: *I want my children to have all the things I've had, but no more.*

4 Most importantly don't forget the golden rule of child rearing in Australia: you're best not to teach kids too much as that might give them an unfair advantage over others.

Keeping the peace

Overburdened perhaps with the drudgery of house-work, mothers in Europe often allow their families to get out of control. Husbands, children, relatives are all permitted to go about unchecked as they give free vent to their egos. The result is heated arguments, noisy exchanges and extended family discussions on every imaginable topic. Brought up in such a bellicose environment, young Europeans soon become outspoken, and confident, with strong personalities of their own.

Australian mothers would never permit such lawlessness.

An Australian mother knows only too well that the family is a volatile institution upon whose unruly members she must exercise a steadying influence. She also knows it is up to her to be peacekeeper if they are not to plunge into anarchy and barbarism through the unchecked and dangerous practices of open argument, face-to-face conflict and general discussion of ideas, subversive to the welfare of the clan.

The process of *keeping the peace* within the clan is a difficult operation and any woman with plans to start a family will have to learn to perform several complicated manouvres worthy of a seasoned diplomat:

1 To run the family properly along Australian lines, your first task must be to keep the various family members, i.e. sons, daughters, spouse, etc., as far apart from each other as possible, so that not even a hint of

conflict may ensue between them. Lines towards this end are:

"Don't bother your father."

"Leave the kids alone."

"You better tell me first."

"You're upsetting your sister."

"No arguing in this house now."

You will have to do this from early childhood on, otherwise some deep attachments could appear which, later on, might lead to all kinds of complications.

2 The job of the peacekeeper is not only to ascertain that family members don't get close enough to one another to have any kind of contact, but also to ensure that if, by chance, trouble *does* ensue, it doesn't ever get resolved. Such resolutions, after all, could lead everyone into uncharted territory.

"Stop it both of you!"

"I don't want to hear any more about it!"

"I think you two better stay away from each other."

The advantage of unresolved conflicts is to ensure that generations of good Australians grow up without knowing how to argue and then make up. This intransigent attitude has also the added advantage of training everyone to live with a general sense of unease and tension from childhood on.

3 Your ultimate aim will be to discourage any kind of exchange of views, whether personal or general, since all such exchanges can potentially lead to a full-blown drama. Even though the family insist that it's only a game that they play, you never know, things can get out of hand.

The reaction to any healthy European-style argument should always be:

"Oh my God, the family's falling apart!"

"I knew it would come to this."

"What am I going to do now?"

"Why can't we just have peace?"

Do not be discouraged by the difficulties you might encounter. With practice the deft hand of the manipulator will become undetectable and you'll be able to work miracles for years to come without ever being sprung.

How to be no trouble

The most important attribute of any child in Australia. Don't get confused by overseas notions that children must actually do something for their parents to be proud of them. In Australia the highest praise you can give any youngster is to deem it *no trouble*. This must be pointed out at every opportunity.

For Good Children

"Oh, Kim's never any problem."
"Aren't you lucky!"
"You'd hardly know Kerry was there."
"Oh, isn't that nice."
"We certainly don't hear a peep out of Ronnie."
"Wonderful!"
"And Tom's a perfect angel."
"I don't know how you do it."

Conversely, you must always point out how much trouble your neighbours, or cousins, or sisters are having with their particular brood.

For Bad Children

"Her Robyn's forever making a racket at the piano."
"Isn't that awful!"
"The flat's always messed up with Dana's chemistry set."
"Oh dear, how dangerous!"
"I don't know how they put up with Lynn's singing."
"Must be dreadful."

155

"Oh, Kenny's a perfect angel, he's no trouble at all!"

"And then there's Ricky who never stops asking questions about the family."

"It just goes to show…"

Overseas parents are forever talking about their children's peculiar ambitions and about how much they have to do to turn the kids into computer geniuses, concert pianists and champion gymnasts. Australian parents, level-headed and naturally modest folk, feel a strong distaste for this kind of overt behaviour and simply will not be part of any such pushiness and presumption.

After all, children may have their own personalities, they may even have special talents, but they shouldn't be allowed to exercise them at the expense of everyone else.

Several years ago, when I was still new to Australia's ways, I was told by a couple at a party: "Oh, we are very proud of our children, they're no trouble at all."

My immediate reaction was to congratulate them. I imagined a pair of brilliant young musicians practising all day long with the encouragement of their parents, or better even, two young electronics wizards preparing themselves for the 21st century.

It was not for some time that I learnt the true meaning of those words. The description of the children as "no trouble" simply meant that the kids:

(a) didn't do anything in particular;

(b) stayed out of their parents' hair;

(c) never spoke unless they were spoken to;

(d) spent a lot of time out of the home in pinball palours; and

(e) in the evenings sat around for hours staring into thin TV.

The twilight zone

Old people in Greece or the Middle East are always expected to live in the same house with their sons and daughters. There they are continually subjected to various pressures like having to cope with boisterous grandchildren who not only expect the poor aged folk to amuse and entertain them, but also ask innumerable painful questions about the past, lost youth or dead friends.

In the Caucasus or Spain, the elderly are even expected to work up to twelve hours a day, well into their late eighties. Trudging up and down hills, shuffling in and out of vineyards and farmyards, forced in the evenings to preside over long dinners with large demanding families who perennially expect help or advice, the old people in these countries just know no rest.

Here in Australia the elderly are dealt with in a much more humane way. Australia, being a modern and progressive society, aims to provide those in their twilight years with a calm, worry-free existence. For this reason steps are taken from the outset to protect the aged from any possible abuse or exploitation by their families.

Following years of study and experience, it has been discovered that the best way to achieve this is to gather the elderly together and keep them safely (and securely) ensconced in one place, under the care of strangers.

Amazingly enough, the best environment for this purpose has been found to be an institution known as

"Ah, come on, Mum and Dad, it's only for the next twenty or thirty years!"

the Nursing Home*. Often built in the grounds of an abandoned mansion, such a home-away-from-home usually consists of many small rooms (not all of them in need of a coat of paint), one large verandah or sunroom with two or three TV sets and corridors just wide enough to permit the free flow of wheelchairs.

The Nursing Home's advantages are obvious. Here the elderly:

- can look forward to peaceful medicated sleep without the danger of being woken early by kids running around the house

- don't have to suffer the stresses of a generation gap since they are exclusively with people of their own age group

- don't have to answer questions

- are away from the prying eyes of a cruel young world

- may spend their final twenty or thirty years in unhurried serenity and without any stimuli whatever.

After a certain point you have to start getting your parents used to the idea of spending their remaining decades in such a dignified environment. *The general idea is to explain that you are sending them to a place where you will be out of their hair.*

Explain clearly and authoritatively that here you will not cause them any more problems than they already have. It's also a good idea to embark on their re-education programmes well in advance, and the following pointers should help:

1 From about 40 onwards, encourage parents to cut down on mixing with younger people. They should start attending bingo nights or lawn bowls instead.

*A name often changed by deed poll to "Retirement Village"

2 Strongly discourage them from spending time at your place. Point out what fun they could have in an environment exclusively of their own generation.

3 Visit them at fewer and fewer intervals so that eventually, except for a couple of hours on Christmas Day, they won't ever have to see their family again.

The natural Australian

The Australian version of the ying and yang. It's all about harmony. Being true to yourself. Being effortless. Flowing with the effluent.

Life must be natural and easy.

And in order to have an Australian-style, effortless, natural life, you only have to remember a few points:

It is natural to be sullen, non-communicative and upset if anyone asks you to do anything; it is natural to assume that others will recall nothing of your last conversation; it is natural not to remember people especially as they're very likely not to remember you; it is natural not to go out of your way to do things.

Spontaneity is NOT natural, a person displaying spontaneous behaviour is considered an irritating artificial performer.

When Australian men are being natural, they want you to acknowledge the fact, i.e. that they're being charming. For this reason when natural Australians meet each other they know to acknowledge the special effort they're both making.

"I thought you were a real bludger but since I got to know you, you're okay."

"Isn't that funny, because I thought you were a real skite, but you're just an ordinary bloke."

For the Australian woman practising being natural is rather different. She is expected to be either sullen or have a high-pitched laugh. Being sullen indicates that

162

she is naturally serious. A high-pitched laugh signifies that she is frivolously natural.

Children should only be allowed to behave one way: naturally.

"Look into the camera, Emma. Be natural. Smile."

NATURAL HIM: Ya know when I first saw ya I thought you were a bit of a slut.

NATURAL HER: Yeah, to tell you the truth I thought you were a bit of a creep too.

In Australia it is considered natural not to know very much, not to say much and not to show your feelings.

Being tense before sex is natural. Being tense after sex is even more so.

It is natural to keep telling people how natural you are.

*"Look, Dad, we've told you — it's 7 bucks
for a wax'n polish and 4 for the tyre black."*

Growing up normal

Since Australia is a land of the future, great emphasis is placed upon the young. In the worn-out, tired societies of Europe, children are merely forced to conform with established patterns. Here all patterns have been dispensed with. Now you have a chance to grow up freely and be yourself, provided you take note of a few simple hints.

1 Make sure you get paid for even the tiniest bit of work you may do for your parents. Grumble about the money they give you. Irrespective of the amount, always demand more. This way you'll get an early understanding of the wage arbitration system.

2 There must be tension between yourself and the rest of the family at all times. The slightest request from parents must produce irritation. Ensure they comprehend that everything you do for them is a real effort.

3 Never show enthusiasm. People might misunderstand and think that you're drunk or on drugs. Besides, you'll save heaps of energy. If you must be enthusiastic about something, it should always be about your *own* plans, projects or ideas, because in Australia this is what "enthusiasm" is usually taken to mean.

4 At school never act too intelligent as that will single you out. If you happen to know the answer to a question, best to keep quiet about it so dumber friends won't think that there is something funny about you.

5 Make your elders happy by not having a point of view of your own. Most Australian grown-ups don't like contradiction. Just repeat what they want to hear and they'll be very grateful to you. Refrain from making any decisions yourself. Ideal types of conversation with adults ought to be:
   "Do you want lunch?"
   "If you like."
   "How hungry are you?"
   "I'm not sure."

6 The last people in the world you should tell your problems to are your father and mother because they already have plenty of worries as things are. It's bad enough that you were born so young and with so little sympathy for their situation, you shouldn't have to trouble them as well.

7 Don't ever expect your family to be one hundred percent behind you because that is not the Australian way. When your parents take the side of teachers, friends, relatives or the police against you, they are simply preparing you for the hardships of the real world ahead.

How to recognise your father

The Australian family's run strictly along British parliamentary lines.

Father is like the country's Governor-General. Hardly recognizable except for his uniform, and seen only at special celebrations, he makes long-winded speeches which he knows are not going to make an iota of difference.

Mother operates like a modern Prime Minister. Expected to make important unpopular decisions but always promising to review the situation at a later date, she tries to remain in power for as long as possible.

Children represent the Opposition. Heard only after much whingeing, shouting and stamping of feet, they feel permanently frustrated and are critical of all family decisions as a matter of course.

Thus, on most days, one may see *mother* taunted by the Opposition across the kitchen table, or the Prime Minister cajoling *father* into signing any number of bills, while on rare occasions *children* might even get to hold the Governor-General's hand.

All patriotic Australians abide by these roles, knowing that attempts to trespass them could plunge the whole family unit into a constitutional crisis.

Hints for the young

1 If you are a nice little girl or boy, you should never talk to anyone in the street, even if they are your grandparents. It's best if you ignore them or set the dog on them. Until you are at least 55 years old and too ancient to be of interest to anyone, you will not be able to judge whether a person is trustworthy or not.

2 Never hold your Dad's hand for more than a couple of seconds, and even then make sure you follow it with a quick jab in the stomach. If you find that your Dad does show more feeling for you than natural (i.e. never), make sure you tell your Mum about it and she'll stick up for you.

3 Never touch your friends. What will people think?

4 Physical affection can also lead to evils like emotional dependence. Your Mummy and Daddy, who know best from experience, will be able to tell you that those who like people, get hurt! If you have to put your arm around something, it's best to put it around a beer bottle.

Father's Day

Being a father involves much the same liabilities all over the world. To be woken by a crying baby in a hut on the Congo is no more romantic than coping with a houseful of screaming infants in Canberra. Waiting up for a teenage daughter till 2 am is equally anxiety provoking in Melbourne and Montevideo. Scraping together enough to pay for the children's tuition carries about the same emotional gratification in Atlantic City as in Adelaide.

But being a father in Australia does present a number of extra responsibilities and duties not found on other parts of the globe, obligations which all Australian fathers have to remember.

Firstly, it's wise when bringing up children in Australia to discourage them from wanting to communicate with you. Ensure that the kids give you a wide berth at all times. Most Australian dads have realized for some time now that the best way to foster their children's development is not to talk to them at all. Difficult as this may seem to practise, you must realize that it is for the good of the kids if the contact between them and yourself is reduced to an absolute minimum. The advantages are obvious:

(a) You won't make any mistakes in their education.

(b) There won't be any dependency on each other.

Going over the top for Dad

(c) Children will eventually learn to become like gum-trees on the edge of a desert — self-reliant and isolated.

As an Australian father you are in a difficult position. You must sire your children and then never put in any further effort in case you confuse them. In fact, Australian fatherhood should be effortless. Sort of like weed-free gardening.

Make liberal use of the back-up services at your disposal and leave the moulding of the children entirely to:

- their mother
- their school-teachers
- the occasional child-welfare officer
- the manager of the local pin-ball parlour

It's important that you should also breed tension in the children because it will help them cope with friends, colleagues and employers later on in life. Here are a few simple techniques to help you maintain the optimum level of tension all year round:

(a) Should the children want something, you must automatically say "no" then walk out of the room.

(b) No matter what, always look at them disapprovingly, as if they had done something wrong.

(c) Never make it clear to anybody whether or not you are angry, upset, pleased or hurt by what they've done.

Naturally, even with a lot of antipodean restraint, things that need to be said between a father and his kids accumulate over the course of time. For this purpose Father's Day was designated as a special day in the

171

Australian calendar.

On Father's Day, after a year of distant glaring, you are permitted at last to talk to the children. You may now shake hands, accept gifts and, in the presence of witnesses, converse freely about accumulated concerns.

"How's it going?"

"Good, Dad."

"Everything OK?"

"Oh, yeah."

"That's all right then."

Remember, though. The rest of the year you must remain a silent enigma.

The Antipodean wedding

The world is familiar with the colourful traditions of Jewish and Greek weddings. Glasses and plates are broken, elaborate rituals accompany every word and there's a great deal of chanting. Not to be outdone, Australians too have devised a complex wedding ritual, as rich in meaning and prescribed behaviour as anything you'll find among the Berbers of the Atlas Mountains or the Uzbeks of Tadjikistan.

Traditionally, each aspect of an Australian wedding constitutes a different struggle. Each planned stage leading up to the actual tying of the matrimonial knot must be the source of acrimonious fights between both bride and groom and their respective anxious families.

"I'm not having Peter as the best man."

"But he's my brother!"

"He's an airline steward!"

"Mum and Dad will be disappointed."

"What about *my* Mum and Dad?"

"They hate me anyway!"

"Because you won't be nice to them!"

As this is a frontier country with a strong pioneering background, such arguments are symbolic representations of the fighting spirit that typifies the Australian way of life.

Every step of the preparations, the date, the venue, the guest list, the presents, the food, the wine list, height of the wedding cake, who should be bridesmaid, who should be best man, what the weather's going to be like, why the wedding should be held in the first place, ought therefore to be the source of a new conflict.

Make sure the bride and groom have their own chance to be directly involved in the conflict every step of the way.

The guest list

Start by disagreeing on the number of guests to be invited. If one wants an intimate ceremony, declare that it's only out of meanness. If the wedding is planned for oodles of people, object to it on the grounds that it voids the intimate sense of marriage.

Neither side ought to like the other one's relatives or friends. Deprecate everyone suggested for invitation on the basis of job, manners, religion, or of what they said back at the engagement party. Threaten to call the whole thing off if the Lismore branch is coming.

The venue

If the other party wants the wedding at home, suggest an expensive hotel. Should they opt for the local RSL Club insist on a lavish restaurant. Argue for several weeks over the issue. Phone up and leave disturbing messages for one another. In the end settle on an asbestos lined community hall down the road, which though too narrow and too dark, is the only venue available for the set date.

The band

If the opposite side demand "young" music, put your foot down and make it clear that a wedding's not a wedding without a traditional band. If the foe wants mushy music to please the older generation, press for a modern raucous pop group.

Fight up to the last minute then hire a makeshift three piece orchestra, or four relatives, or a gaggle of professional musicians who've never played together before. Ensure there is a "singing" drunken uncle close on hand who can embarrass half the hall and anger the rest.

The food

For a REAL Australian wedding the fare has to be awful. This shouldn't be difficult to achieve once everyone agrees to disagree over the culinary details.

If the groom's crowd want everything catered, insist on the necessity of having home cooked food. Explain that you couldn't possibly disappoint Aunt Dot whose specialty is asparagus rolled in crustless bread with a toothpick through it. Nor can you let down Cousin Joyce who does wonders with pineapple rings and apple-pie-a-la-mode.*

If the bride's folks *do* decide to have the wedding lavishly catered, try to squeeze in as many of the groom's family and friends into the reception as you can. Point out that they *are* all your best mates and that they *did* invite you to *their* weddings. If this doesn't work, make a long list of allergy sufferers in the family who will need specially prepared meals.

Make sure you don't serve anchovies or anything smelly.

The drinks

The bride's kin ought to demand sophisticated drinks to go with the lovely dishes. This should cause a lot of trouble because drinks, traditionally, end up costing more than the food.

The groom's side, on the other hand, should announce loud and clear that since the bride's lot are just a bunch of drunkards, beer and extra-sweet sparkling wine will do just nicely.

---

* A la mode in Australia usually means with a dob of aerosol whipped cream.

In revenge, the bride's relations can always make sure that the beer-cooling Temprite on the keg does not work properly, and that the carpet (or lawn) gets covered in a nice thick layer of froth.*

The cake

The *pièce de résistance*, of course.

It's never nice. Bake it well in advance to ensure just the right sort of dryness. This is a wonderful opportunity for future in-laws to join in a lively slanging match.

"Looks too rich for me."

"It's not *very* moist."

"If only they used my recipe."

"What a disappointment!"

"It's what comes from skimping."

All guests can now contribute by making snide remarks. Clan barriers break down and in matters of resentment it's everyone for themselves. Remember that the aim is to give the young couple a foretaste of the fighting spirit that has made Australia what she is today.

"You'd think they'd go to more trouble."

"He never even said thank you."

"Fancy seating me with that lot."

"I knew I spent too much on the present."

"I thought she'd end up with better than him."

And that classic of Australian classics:

"They've left us with all the mess!"

* *Known as "Tampering with the Temprite".*

Visions in fruitcake.

The bedroom, the loungeroom

A poet once called the eyes "the mirrors of the soul". Evidently he wasn't Australian. Australians learn early from their parents that the real mirror of the soul is the state of one's bedroom.

They learn that the more unused and deserted a bedroom appears, the better impression its owners will make on the world. The bedrooms Australians admire the most, in fact, are those which look as if their occupants slept elsewhere.

To create an environment, therefore, where your partner or occasional visitor will feel comfortable, you must put all old-fashioned notions of decorating aside and take as your inspiration — the motel room.

Go for the unlived-in look. Keep everything out of sight. A bedroom should never be tainted by the identity of those inhabiting it. This is a courteous society and it is bad manners to have a personality of one's own.

Things private must be safely stowed away. It's best to give bedrooms a rigid and uninviting appearance. Eradicate any hint of their real purpose. Make sure beds are all made up by 7 am to discourage those who might want to use them again.

A well-designed home in Australia ought to be able to trap any would-be visitors at the front door, and then keep them there for as long as possible or until they decide to go away.

Any soundly built house must also be able to encourage relatives, and especially friends, to enter through the back door so that they may get ensnared in the kitchen. This is where most social activities occur.

The loungeroom is the last place you take people into. Unfortunately, there *are* rare occasions when you're forced to use the loungeroom. Here are a few handy hints to ensure that the guests' sojourn there is of minimum length:

1 Ensure the loungeroom has a stale ambience so guests won't want to stay.

2 Loungeroom furniture ought to appear cemented in or bolted down. Create the impression that should any item be moved a centimetre either way, the owners would feel incredible personal distress.

3 Push sofas, chairs and settees against the walls so that visitors have to sit a long way from each other. This prevents any undue intimacy and discourages relaxing.

4 Place coffee tables either too close to allow people to stretch out their legs or otherwise just out of reach.

5 Leave huge empty spaces in the middle of the room. This facilitates vacuuming and also reproduces the perimetric life-style of the Australian continent.

Renovations

Most renovations in Australia begin innocuously enough. The home, no matter how lovely, comfortable or expensive, suddenly proves inadequate for living in. If only there were a small door here, a wider window there, a kitchen sink on the opposite wall and slate tiles in the bathroom — if only these things were done, then the home would surely be perfect.

But sadly, irrespective of where you put the new patio, sink, toilet bowl, spare room or open fire-place, someone (spouse, relatives or friends) will explain to you most patiently that these things should not have been placed *there*. On the roof, yes, in the backyard maybe, or hanging above the front gate; anywhere, in fact, but not where *you* had decided to place them.

Events now get out of control. The renovations soon spread to the entire household and take over large chunks of the people's lives.

There's cement in the carpets, paint marks on the curtains, tacks and nails between sofa cushions, sudden cracks above the staircase, nastily scratched window panes, bits missing out of doorways, permanently grubby taps, mysteriously broken vases, chandeliers hanging by single threads of wire, laundries filled with rubble, garden-beds smothered by bricks, corridors that become impassable for months.

Could all this chaos be accidental?

Far from being haphazard, renovations in Australia follow a clear and traceable pattern. Research has shown that each stage of a renovation bears, in fact, a strong correlation to the marital problems of those undertaking it:

ADDITIONAL STOREY TO SUBURBAN HOME	Couple would prefer divorce but can't afford it
BACKYARD SHED TURNED INTO DEN	Husband caught up in mid-life crisis but too afraid to have outside liaisons
EXTENDING THE LOUNGEROOM	Wife trying to keep husband suspected of having affairs at home
SEPARATE DINING AREA CREATED	Marriage in socio-economic rut, wife dreams of mixing with people above her station
NEW BATHROOM	Husband dissatisfied with sex-life; wife approaching menopause
NEW KITCHEN AND BUILT-INS	Marriage on the rocks — wife threatens to walk out
MODERNIZING NARROW WINDOWS	Spouses fancy some infidelity but haven't found right person
WHOLE HOUSE REDECORATED	Couples have simply given up on each other and lead separate lives

Be warned, however. If you wish to keep the marriage going, do not complete renovations. Leave bits of construction work permanently unfinished. It may be anything from a few missing tiles under the sink to a huge gap in the back wall.

In Australia experience has shown that once renovations are completed, and there are no other possible improvements to be made, the property somehow always ends up being sold.

The solitude of separation.

Networking your divorce

IF you want to make it big in Australia then you must consider divorce. Divorce is at the basis of the Australian business experience. Like owning your first car or buying your first property, your divorce provides that all-important training ground for dealings with the legal, accounting and banking professions.

There are several stages needed to expand your network of contacts.

Stage 1. Two children and seven years down the track you take a look at your partner and realise that things aren't what they used to be. One morning over breakfast you bring up the topic of divorce.

> *Spouse:* But I thought we were happy.
> *You:* I did too.

Stage 2. After a few sessions with an impartial certified accountant and an amiable tax consultant, both sides accept that temporary separation is the best possible course of action. He agrees to give her an allowance and one of the two cars. She agrees that he has free access to their children and joint bank account.

> *One:* You take the leather Chesterfield.
> *The Other:* No, no, you take it.
> *One:* I insist.
> *The Other:* I think you need it more.
> *One:* Okay, but then I want you to have the Parker dining room suite.

> **The Other:** You love music more than I do. I insist you take the Aiwa.
>
> **One:** All right, but you should keep the Blaupunkt.
>
> **The Other:** We are both going to be happy with our new decision.
>
> **One:** Life is going to be better for everyone all around.
>
> **The Other:** And we are both going to stay good friends.

Stage 3. Within two months of attending self-improvement and physical fitness classes, one has found a better and more highly paid job and the other has found somebody ten years younger, fresher and lovelier. Now it really starts.

> **She:** He's a bad influence on the children. (*Promptly refuses access and takes the kids to the country where he can't get at them*)
>
> **He:** She doesn't really need the car. I'd rather give it to my new girlfriend. (*Sneaks around one night and drives it away with a set of spare keys*)

Stage 4. On advice from a unbiased marriage counsellor, he spends endless amounts of time looking for receipts to prove that things were bought before they got married. On advice from an understanding psychiatrist, she gets people to search for secret bank accounts she knows he's got hidden somewhere.

> **She:** I'll teach him a lesson he'll never forget!
>
> **He:** I'd rather burn the sofa than let her have it!

Stage 5. Urged by a successful solicitor he tries to have himself declared bankrupt in order not to have to give her any money. She is still searching for his hidden bank accounts and, advised by a sympathetic magistrate, has the kids placed under police protection.

Stage 6. Divorce is now all the go and the respective brilliant barristers are demanding everything for their clients. The family court judge like Solomon decides to split the assets down the middle.

> One: (*With venom*) Very well, I'll have A to K of
>   the Britannica set, you can have L to Z.
> The Other: (*With hatred*) OK, I'll have the insides of the
>   piano and you can have the case.

Finally, it is necessary to sell the house and all the other assets anyway, in order to pay for the costs. But in the meantime the network of solicitors, barristers, removalists, analysts, guidance counsellors, think-positive teachers, physical education instructors, accountants, baby-sitters, private detectives and assorted financial advisors have become your permanent business connections, if not your life-long friends. For many, of course, divorce is often the first *and* last business experience.

How to make an Australian sandwich

In Germany, if you wish for a quick snack, someone is sure to fix one up within minutes of your asking. With Teutonic precision, German sandwich-makers will butter a dozen slices of pumpernickel, fill them with Berliner and Bismarck herrings which are always kept in the fridge at the ready, and cut them neatly into halves. It's a fast and uninterrupted blitz.

Naturally in Australia such precision is frowned upon. Australians, a nation of individualists, like to give their sandwich-making that personal touch. Therefore preparing a snack becomes not so much a chore as an expression of the snack-maker's inner thermos. Rather, ethos.

Once you too have decided to be an individualist, you're ready to make an Australian sandwich. Once you've mastered this, improvisation and mayonnaise may freely flow. Here then are the basic steps to follow.

Remove Tip Top from Westinghouse. Take two to six slices out, keep them in hand, and wander around kitchen trying to locate a Noritake plate. Place slices on edge of stove to answer the telephone. Back in kitchen, remember tin of Golden Circle stored in corner of colonial-style smooth edge cupboard. Place Golden Circle on top of TV Week.

Pick up bread from edge of stove and rummage for Staysharp knife behind stack of Tupperware. Spread Norco on bread. Light a cigarette. Catch glimpse of interesting article in TV Week lying on table. Take Golden Circle from top of magazine stack and place on edge of stove, buttered slices on Knebel bench, unbuttered ones on K-tel Kitchenmate, loaf of Tip Top back into Westinghouse, Staysharp on table. Finish reading TV Week.

Transfer buttered slices from bench to table. Move stack of Women's Weeklies and old TV Weeks to sideboard to make room. Transfer boiled eggs from fridge to edge of sink. Notice patchily buttered slices and spread Norco to same evenness throughout. Transfer Staysharp to bench.

Take plate off table and move it closer to buttered slices on bench. Locate last Vegemite jar behind tins of Pal. Hold Vegemite under hot water to loosen lid. Look around for Staysharp to prize lid open. Transfer magazines from sideboard to sink, convinced that knife has fallen behind them. (In fact it's under the plate on the bench.)

Mix Lea & Perrins curry powder. Look for eggs. Salvage from under stack of Women's Weeklies on edge of sink. Attempt to light another cigarette. Replace flint in Dunhill lighter. Move buttered bread, Vegemite, squashed eggs and Golden Circle to table. TV Weeks back to sideboard, Staysharp into sink.

Sit down exhausted. Get up again. Put teaspoon of Nescafe into cup, add sugar and Longlife milk. Put into Toshiba microwave, sit down again, and watch the boiling coffee turning slowly around.

You're now ready to make that sandwich.

Helping out one's mates

As inheritors in the main of an Anglo-Saxon culture, Australians have a deep respect for the democratic ways of life. This means that they feel no sympathy for the money grabbing, avaricious and unpleasant habits prevalent in other countries.

Take, for instance, corruption.

When an Italian pays a Mafia member to get his son off military service, it is, undoubtedly, bribery. When a Chinese gives a large sum of money to a Party official to get him a bicycle ahead of 100,000 others, that too is called bribery. When an Australian slips some money to someone to get his brother off a drink-driving charge, he is not bribing anybody. He is simply making a donation.

Straight out bribery is a foreign habit, practised by grubby, self-motivated people with slicked-back hair and hirsute fingers, who live in faraway lands. Donations, no matter to what obscure causes, are sunny, kind, charitable and typically Australian.

Naturally, an Australian in trouble will want to find the way out of it as much as any Peruvian or Frenchman. It also goes without saying that there are ways of attenuating one's woes — but never at the expense of jeopardising one thousand years of built-in, Anglo-Saxon respect for the law.

That is why an Australian may "help out a mate", he* may "do someone a favour", he may even "push another's cause", and if it is "made worth his while", he might even "stick his neck out for you", or "bend the

*Women appear to be precluded from the use of the word "mate".

188

Helping out one's mates

rules a little". He knows that what he is doing could never possibly be called corruption.

After all, "corrupt" countries are run by greasy dictators aided by fat officials in shiny suits and with heavy accents, who take the whole thing very seriously — in a style far removed from the light-hearted, matey, easy going Australian way.

So what you must do, in trying to extricate yourself from trouble, is look around for someone who'll give you a knowing wink and an understanding response like:

"I've got a mate who might be able to help you."

"I know this great bloke who's never let down a mate yet."

"What you want is a little mate with the right connections."

This is the cue. The moment a mate, or a mate's capacity, is mentioned, you know that you are on the right track. Chances of clambering out of trouble have now greatly increased, and you should welcome the other person's offer with laughing snorts and some light-hearted frivolity.

"D'you reckon he'll want to help a geezer like me? Heh! Heh! Heh!"

"Ah, well, you might have to make it worth his while. After all, he's got to come in from Vaucluse! Hah! Hah! Hah!"

A slightly derisory and jovial attitude is necessary as proof that this is neither corruption nor an illegal connivance, but really a kindly turn, a friendly game between mates, who are basically superior to any dirty and deliberate breaking of the law.

The national industry

EVERY country worthy of being called a nation possesses one particular industry that provides people with the main source not only of their revenue but also of their civic pride. In Nauru the national industry is mining bird droppings rich in superphosphate. In Taiwan, assembling half-priced American-style computers. In Rumania, pickling and bottling gherkins.

In Australia the national industry is cheating the government.

This high-growth enterprise with a rate of expansion that is the envy of the Western World provides both direct and indirect employment to a huge section of the population. Company directors and receptionists, accountants and bankrupts, plumbers and doctors, artists and dock workers, lawyers and criminals, butchers and politicians, financial advisors and little old ladies, all toil to make the Australian national industry what it is today.

The national industry will look after you from the time you leave school till well after retiring age. No matter how small the scale you begin with, you can soon find a profitable niche depending on your interests and ingenuity.

"How did you go this year?"

"I managed to claim for my daughter's pet wombat."

"Yeah, well, next time you should go the whole hog."

Do not get fooled by the old adage: "Nothing is certain in the world except for death and taxes." Though the first claim might yet be investigated (sometimes a miraculous revivification has taken place of individuals long thought dead who reappeared magically to head small mining consortiums in Western Australia), the second one has definitely been proved wrong due to the concerted dedication of Australians, so that the adage now reads: "Only two things are certain in Australia, death and tax fiddles."

The sharpest and most daring have made a dramatic discovery. Known as the Australian Taxation Corollary it dictates that the larger your company, the less the amount of payable tax. Conversely, the smaller the company, the greater the amount of deductions. The corollary also states that tax can be paid in two basic ways:

(a) As little as possible.

(b) None at all.

Remember that no matter how paltry the fiddle you begin with, this is a country of limitless opportunities and your own success in the national industry depends merely on the confines of your boldness. While in other parts of the world experts may believe that the last word in tax rorts has been spoken, Australians from all walks of life dedicate more energy to cheating the government than to any other national endeavour.

A considerable part of your time ought to be spent not only hiding your true earnings from the government but also inventing persons earning them. It's important that you should do business or be employed under various names in order to increase the size of Australia's working population. Humble but hard-working Australians apply themselves very seriously to this task.

"If someone rings for Phil say I'm at the brewery."

"All right."

"If they ask for Ron tell them I've gone to get the bricks."

"Very well."

"If a woman wants Bill find out the age of the car."

"Fine."

"And if they inquire after Bob say I've bought the pipes."

"Great."

"And if you want me at the factory better ask for Mac."

"OK."

"Now are you sure you can remember all that?"

"No worries, Grandpa."

This technique may be applied especially to the field of social security benefits, compensation and welfare. Apply for assistance under three or four names in order to keep the industry buoyant. With a little effort it is possible to simultaneously work under one name while claiming under several others a permanent disability pension for an incapacitated spine, and live in public housing while you are paying off your home.

Not only are the nine governments of Australia willing to encourage the national industry, successful industry members also never miss an opportunity to claim assistance with some cashgrant from one government or another. The country is full of individuals with a long established knowledge in the field and it would be wise to trust yourself to one of these experts to guide you through the many available avenues.

"I understand you can help me obtain a government cash-grant."

"Have you a farm?"

"I don't think so."

"Don't worry, I've six people ready to swear that you've got one."

"Why?"

"Because the government likes people to have bilberry farms and is willing to pay for the privilege of seeing people establishing them."

"I see."

"And very few have claimed for farms this year."

"Oh."

"And the money set aside for them could easily get lost."

"So?"

"So to save the government the wastage..."

Modern-day pioneers from all over the globe, lured

by the glitter of Australia's national industry, are also keen to be part of the action. Like the bounty-hunters of old who roamed the Wild West, a great number of New Zealanders, British, Americans, Germans, Chinese and Japanese criss-cross the seven states of Australia in audacious search of generous government endowments.

"What do you mean a floating dock subsidy?"

"I only need help of a hundred thousand."

"But you're an hour's drive from Alice Springs!"

"All right, fifty thousand."

"And your registered company address is a hut in the desert!"

"Very well, I'll settle for twenty-five."

"And the only water for miles is subterranean!"

"OK, for ten thousand I'll build it underground."

How to be respectable

To earn people's respect in England you'd do well to marry into a family with a long lineage. In Italy it's best to become involved in one of the political parties. Respect in most Arab countries is earned by praying in a mosque five times a day.

If you want to be respected in Australia, you must become a heavy, committed gambler.

Australians have a great admiration for gamblers and see them as embodiments of the national ethos, much like the way the Swiss regard their more established bankers. They realise that more than a flag, an anthem or a coast-to-coast highway, a nation gambling as one will always be united against all odds.

Unimaginative Europeans, brought up to regard gambling as wasteful, fail to see how risking a large percentage of one's weekly income on a horse running 3000 kms away, can be an expression of one's respectability. Australians, of course, know better. They were the first nation to break through old-world taboos. Far from apologising for it, they've made gambling the cornerstone of their nationhood and use it the way Popes used religion to unite medieval Europe. An intricate network covers the country for this purpose:

Racecourses, dog tracks, poker machines, lottery agencies, two-up schools, TAB offices, SP shops, bingo houses, trotting meets, stock exchanges, futures markets, art-union mailouts, church raffles, write-in competitions, lotto promotions, luxury casinos, golden caskets, instant prizes, soccer pools, cockroach races and earthworm tournaments.

You may hear in fact mysterious incantations wherever you go:

"Eleven and twenty-five always come up together."

"The third in the fourth looks good."

"I was told I'd only get four to seven on the red in the second but I got on at four to five."

In Europe if you can identify every one of Mozart's symphonies, people will say about you "That person is cultured." Do the same thing in Australia and you'll be called a show-off. Name, however, every horse and rider who's won the Melbourne Cup since 1861 and you will be regarded with great respect.

Talking about race-horses or dogs is never showing off. You are admired as someone worthwhile. It's OK to be interested even in something like computers as long as you intend to use it for working out winners at the track or lucky Lotto numbers.

Men and women who back in Budapest, Zurich or Vienna would have never dreamt of gambling 5 dinars of their hard earned money, and whose parents would have turned white at the thought of their children wasting their wages, in Australia soon shed all inhibitions and devote many waking hours to this new fount of respectability.

It's not as if they're gambling — they're simply trying to gain acceptance. Accountants, lawyers, general practitioners, all do it, purely to be sociable and earn the respect of their clients, of course. Most of the clients are at the races, anyway.

In other countries unenlightened parents are horrified if their children gamble. In Australia, parents keen to see their kids grow up respected members of the community, encourage gambling from an early age.

"Don't waste your money, Bev! Better buy Lotto!"

"Grandpa reckons Concerto is set to win."

"I bought everyone scratchies for Christmas but gave Mum an Opera House and Dad a Systems Seven."

It's important, therefore, to train children from an early age to buy lotteries for birthdays, hold intra-family Melbourne Cup sweeps, organize clan nights at the pokies, watch Lotto results gathered around the telly, and to put into practice the wise old dictum: *the family that bets together, gets together.*

"I got my owner an Order of Australia. What did you get yours?"

How to react to the police

You have to exhibit a certain amount of fear. Police become very suspicious of people who do not show some anxiety. Even police get anxious when they run into other police.

It's advisable to act tense to prove that you are innocent. All the guilty people, who have much more time to watch phoney TV police shows, tend to act really relaxed. The way to achieve the tense look is to tell yourself, the moment you see a blue uniform:

"Ah, there's the police. I must be doing something wrong."

If you happen to come from a Continental type environment where a healthy disregard for the law has been the practice for the past few hundred years, then the best way to inspire fear in yourself at the sight of the police is to think thoughts such as:

"Maybe paying $75 for that new 26-inch stereo TV *was* a bit cheap . . ."

"I wonder if the bond money on that old flat *did* cover the last four weeks' rent?"

Though this system is partially effective, it still cannot bring police and the general public closer together. Unfortunately, the only people in Australia who understand the police are the criminals. But that's only natural since they spend so much time together.

Even police are scared of police . . .

Understanding a Fair Go

While the French produced the baffling ideas of Existentialism and the Germans discovered the potent laws of Dialectics, Australians were also busy, giving the world the complex concept of a Fair Go.

The concept of a Fair Go is about giving everyone a chance to make fools of themselves. It is about letting people make mistakes.

For example, if some friends happen to start a small business they know nothing about and you see pitfalls in their initial efforts, it is only fair that you should not warn them against possible disasters lurking around the corner. The laws of Fair Go dictate that you leave them completely on their own.

This, it must be pointed out, should not depress you as by the unwritten laws of a Fair Go, though the business might go bankrupt, your friends can always start again.

Also, by the same rule, should you notice any friends speak of a scheme that might make them rich or famous, it's only equitable that you warn them of the dangers of their own personal ambitions. Philosophical arguments to be used on such occasions are:

"It's already been done."

"The multinationals will get you."

"It's the worst possible time to do it."

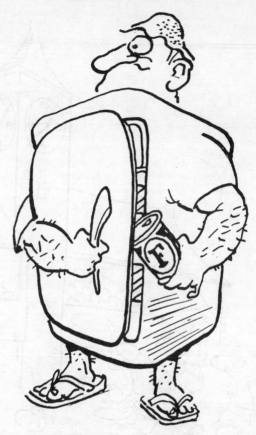

It pays to be self-sufficient

"I know someone who tried and today they're being looked after by the Salvation Army."

Conversely, if you have any worthwhile plans yourself, you ought to keep them as secret as possible — especially from your friends.

No other theory encapsulates so successfully the general Australian outlook on life, which decrees therefore that the person most unsuited and with the least experience gets the job.

A Public Service sort of game

Cricket

The Americans do not have to play cricket because they beat the English, fair and square, in the 1776 War of Independence.

Australians, who have not as yet had the chance to get stuck into the English in open warfare, hang on to cricket, hoping thus to prove themselves the better and the stronger.

Cricket is essentially an agrarian game, designed to give everyone a go. What is rather good about cricket is that it requires the minimum of effort over the maximum amount of time.

Not that much different from working for the Public Service, really. The game doesn't start till about ten, there's a lot of standing around, a fair amount of gossip and rivalry, people break for lunch and tea, and as soon as conditions aren't just ideal, everyone stops.

A friend, new to Australia, after hearing a great deal about the game but never having seen it played, insisted that friends take him along to a match. Once installed in his seat, he ate and drank with his friends, oblivious of the passage of time. Towards late afternoon, however, when the food and beer were beginning to run out, he turned to his friends and said with polite but casual curiosity:

"So tell me, when is this game going to start?"

Fortunately most of the boredom of cricket, for the players at least, has been removed nowadays by widening the game to include the drinking of beer and heavy intoxicating liquor on Australian television commercials.

So as long as you are reasonably intact, without visible

signs of cerebral palsy, and can stand up for seven or eight hours without falling asleep (a ball will fly past you every now and then), your chances of making it through the game are fairly good.

If you also happen to be fairly dull, well-behaved, and have the stomach to drink with the more influential cricket team selectors, your chances of becoming captain of the side are even better.

Should you be willing to forget the inconveniences of travel, or those of standing in a field somewhere in England, the Caribbean or Asia — hoping that whatever flies towards you is a ball and not a bomb — you might in fact become a cricket great, adored by hundreds of thousands of screaming fans.

Patience, after all, makes many things possible. Even becoming a great Australian.

Loyalty Down Under

A NATION is made great by the loyalty of its citizens to a noble and mutual cause.

In Japan you are loyal to the Company. You start each dawn with the eight verses of the Company song, toil hard alongside your colleagues for ten to twelve hours, then drink a litre of sake with the same colleagues after hours till midnight. For your five-day annual holidays you all go away together to a work-motivation camp where you discuss, naturally, the production problems of a company you know you will stay with for the rest of your life.

In Italy, on the other hand, you're loyal to the Family. Yours, that is. One uncle owns the angora goats that another uncle shears and brings to the village where aunts and cousins weave the wool into cashmere, which when brought to town father cuts into patterns which your six brothers and sisters sew into exclusive outfits to be sold around places like Australia under a David Jones label.

In Australia loyalty is seen in a totally different light.

Here allegiance to any *party* is pointless because none of them will provide you with much in the way of luxuries, schools or lodgings, things which, in any case, are more easily obtained in Australia by borrowing money from a bank or credit union. Devotion to the *family* is also superfluous as by staying at home you will only get in the way. Besides, Mum and Dad are already under enough stress from each other. And it's certainly not necessary to show loyalty to the *company* you work for since by moving on to a new position you are not only vacating the job for someone else but reducing unemployment as well.

In Australia your loyalty is to brand-names.

Here words such as Vegemite, Aeroplane Jelly and Violet Crumble inspire the same fervour and arouse the same high adrenalin level that terms like *partiya, famiglia* or *chosei* do to the body chemistry of overseas loyalists.

Just as Poles in exile become all tearful at the sight of the beloved red and white flag of their nation, Australians away from their home country go jelly-like in the knees at the mere sight of a Vegemite red and orange label.

Very early in life children in a place such as Northern Ireland learn to be loyal to the Protestant or Catholic parties of their respective backgrounds. In Nicaragua kids become aware at a tender age that they have to choose between loyalty to the Sandinistas or the Contras. Similarly in Australia, even in isolated outback places, your childhood loyalties are established at a tender age between Kelloggs and Sanitarium, Fountain and Rosella, Cadburys and Nestles, Peters and Streets.

Since Australians are no less fiercely loyal than overseas zealots, if you love Vegemite you simply don't eat Marmite; Monte Carlo aficionados won't have a bar of Iced Vo Vo's; while Fosters drinkers avoid Tooheys like the plague. It's all out war between Brut and Old Spice splashers. Tampax wielders won't go near a Modess. Ansell fans won't touch a Durex with a ten foot pole. Generations of Holden enthusiasts wouldn't be seen dead in a Ford.

Your favourite brand names stay with you for life and allegiance to them proves your steadfastness of character to everyone. Successful persons in Australia always know to trot out their loyalties at the right moment in order to create the correct impression:

"Oh, I've eaten Aeroplane Jelly from the time I was six, and haven't tried anything else ever since."

206

"No matter how poor we were I would only use Kleenex toilet rolls in the bathroom."

"I don't go for any of these fancy cheeses, just give me a slice of Coon."

You are also expected to maintain your brand-name loyalties right through your rise to the top to show that underneath you are really an acceptable, ordinary Australian. Hence though you may drink a French cognac like Courvoisier in private, in public you still go for Vic Bitter or XXXX. And though you may wear an original Swiss-made Rolex, point out that it is held on by your favourite Woolworths watchband.

Resignation

ANYONE can get a job. The real art lies in knowing how to resign.

The Japanese feel a deep obligation to stay with a company for life. In the unlikely event that someone does decide to leave, they will be looked upon as freaks and spoken of with suspicion for the rest of their days.

"Remember Yukiyama?"

"The one who resigned from Sony in '68?"

"'67 to be exact."

"What about him?"

"His son just changed jobs."

"It only goes to show."

"Tarred with the same brush."

"The apple doesn't fall far from its tree."

While not exactly bound for life, Germans sign work-contracts for periods of up to ten years. Those who break their agreements and wish to leave earlier than stipulated must face the consequences.

"Come in, Schmackelpuss."

"Yes, sir."

"I understand you wish to leave five weeks early."

"Yes, sir."

"Here are the necessary resignation forms."

"Where? In this crate?"

"Have them filled in by March."

Australian attitudes to employment are rather different. In Australia, the mobile society par excellence, after three months you are well-respected and established, while a year-long stint in a job makes you practically an old-timer. Anything over three years is looked at with suspicion.

"You've been here a while, haven't you?"

"So have you."

"I'm only staying because they give me a car."

"Oh, well, that's all right then. Me, I'm just saving up to go overseas."

In countries such as Sweden, Holland and the United States, you can improve your position by doing the right things and staying with the company. In Australia you achieve the same result by leaving it.

Conditions under which you should resign are:

(a) You don't like someone.

(b) Someone doesn't like you.

(c) They refuse your third pay rise for the season.

(d) You've stolen enough clients to start a business of your own.

(e) They announce a general audit.

(f) You're about to be fired.

At no time should you show allegiance to either employers, or fellow employees. It's not necessary because you know that by moving on you are vacating the job for someone else. In fact you are creating employment and exercising your freedom at the same time. And since Australia is a mobile society, it is the duty of every conscientious employee to keep on the move.

The French, if they wish for a career, do a step-by-step advance from dumb menial jobs until they become well-rounded professionals with a high degree of expertise. In Australia the only expertise you need is one in changing jobs.

The lead-up to a resignation is always the most crucial period of your employment. It should begin from the moment you take up your new job.

"Things look very suss to me."

"Seems they're really rapt about going broke here."

"I'd be shocked if I can stick it out."

Escalate your grumbling and complaints but be wary to do it only to people who don't matter or who can't help the situation. Clothe your distress in cryptic remarks:

"This place has more problems than a high-school maths book."

"Someone here would rat on her mother's RSI."

Remain in your job only until your first pay rise. That same week start looking for a new position which offers you more money. Should they refuse to give you another increase the way is open for you to resign immediately because they're obviously not paying you what you're worth.

"They're too mean even to hang themselves."

Take care, however, to never actually give the real reasons why you are resigning otherwise problems could get sorted out and you might be forced to stay on.

*"How many times have I told you that my new wage bracket has taken
me beyond a chop and three vegies . . . ?"*

Junking friends

IF your colleague, boss or partner irks you, don't bother to fight it out. There's no need for a slow acrimonious build up of graduated arguments, fights and remonstrations. Just a few brief weeks of mulling and then bingo! a strike, a resignation or a divorce. You must never give warning with little complaints, let alone attempt to sort it out. You must strike suddenly in order to catch the other side unawares and unprepared. Then junk them.

If friends annoy you, don't bother to sort it out. Junk them. If you can't stand the awful sandals one of them wears, or the hairstyle someone adopted, junk them along with the whole group. Look upon the process as a garage sale and make it clear that you're not junking friends for profit but to simplify life. Australians know it's best to travel light. Friends slow you down after a while.

After all, what would you say to a friend whom you are not inviting to a party?

"They're not your crowd."

"I reckon they would make you feel nervous."

"I'd rather meet you on more intimate terms. At a pub."

You should always junk your friends as soon as you change jobs. Your true friends want the best of everything for you and they all realise that there comes a seasonal time when you've got to junk them in order to move up in the world.

Announce that you're holding a spring clean. Since you've got a new job and you are moving to a different location, everything will have to go. Including old friends.

And when someone you haven't seen for a few weeks suddenly confronts you with: "What happened to the crowd I used to see you with?" look serious, communicate your profound regret on the matter with a sigh and reply: "Oh, I've outgrown them" or "I've moved on since then."

It's praiseworthy to junk your whole group of friends, your past, your family, whole suburbs because:

(a) others want to remain in their situation and you don't wish to disturb their peace of mind;

(b) you earn more than they do; and

(c) you are a maturing type serious about success.

Why you shouldn't work in the field you're trained in

PEOPLE in other countries work hard so that they can get somewhere. In Australia people work hard so they can get away from it and do something else.

Australia is a modern and progressive nation where new work ethics apply. You have far greater career prospects if you hate what you do. It means that you are broadminded and open to any offers that may come along. People who claim that they actually enjoy their work and are having fun soon get their comeuppance. They are looked on as narrow-minded and amateurish and not taken seriously at all. This is because as children Australians have been taught that if something is enjoyable then probably it's not only bad for them but weakens their character as well.

As a result Australia is full of architects who hate buildings, farmers who hate the land, publishers who hate books and waiters who hate people.

Proud, freedom-loving beings, Australian workers hate to be thought of as slaves to their profession. To earn the respect of your colleagues, therefore, it's important to always have another out. Make it clear to everyone that though you have a great job you are secretly planning to:

(a) mine for opals at Coober Pedy
(b) run a fishing trawler off Cairns
(c) open a hairdressing shop in Wagga.

Best to look for a job you have no expertise in whatsoever. Remember that Australia is a pioneering

215

nation and here people think it a sign of intelligence to have succeeded in a profession they never trained for.

When choosing an apprenticeship or course of study, pick a field you have no intention at all of being involved in.

BRICKLAYER
MD. PhD. BSc.
BEc. LLB. MA.
DipEd. BA.(Hon)
Telephone: 789890

Australians study, of course, as assiduously as the rest of the world. Everyone is very keen to acquire the profession which they know they are not going to practise. Parents are especially eager for children to do this.

"You should always have a trade, Bianca, to fall back on."

"You never know, Tom, when being a dentist might come in handy."

"It's a good idea to have a few apprenticeships up your sleeve, Trent."

Should you happen to train as an opera conductor there is every chance that your real success will come from the manufacture of plastic sewerage pipes. As a well-trained psychiatrist or pediatrician you owe it to your self-respect to make a fortune on the property market. Should your background be nuclear physics you might try your luck patenting an impermanent tattoo for teenagers. After four years of training as a sailmaker, could you hope for any more self-satisfying job than renovating pubs in Tibooburra?

Or you may choose to change professions several times in a lifetime.

"I've come to complain about the cupboards you installed."

"Sorry, can't help you."

"Aren't you the carpenter?"

"That was last week. I'm into tree surgery now."

"What am I going to do then?"

"Tell you what. I've got a mate I trained with at cookery school who's thinking of giving up his hairdressing practice and getting into home decorating. Why don't you give him a call?"

All in all, your ambition should be to become the complete suburban renaissance person — multi-faceted, multi-talented and multi-jobbed.

How to be moody

The Chinese will always greet you with the same degree of warmth. The Swiss, on the other hand, take a lot of trouble over their surliness, hoping that it will keep them neutral for another 800 years. A Brazilian would not dream of being anything but casual and friendly. In fact, in most places around the Globe, steadiness of temperament is held up to be a virtue.

Australians, however, being a freedom-loving people, do not believe in restricting themselves to such constant behaviour. Instead, as true sons and daughters of the great outdoors, they take their cue for personal relationships from . . . the weather.

In order to be in complete harmony with the elements, Australians have learnt to alter their moods rapidly and without prior warning. Having grown up in the unpredictable climate of the Fifth Continent, they feel that it is unnatural to be constant and that one ought to be suspicious of people who are.

I would advise all Tourists and Newcomers: abandon your old-fashioned constant ways and adopt moodiness as your new method of communication. This will not only repress more successfully those around you, but will also help instil a constant sense of guilt in everyone — a guilt which, being secret, is likely to cement Australian society even closer together.

Like the tropical cyclones that descend on this country out of the blue, moodiness is at its most effective when used for no apparent reason. There should never be any hint of an explanation. Never venture a motive for it.

"You look upset all of a sudden."

"It's nothing."

"Was it something I said?"

"I just realised that I've got to leave. I've got another appointment."

"But you said you had a free afternoon."

"Maybe I have. I'm not sure."

The aim of most moodiness, of course, is tension, tension and more tension. Yoga and other mystical fashions began to lose much of their popularity here when it was discovered that, with their emphasis on relaxation, they were cutting into people's moodiness and causing highly suspicious behaviour.

"You laughing at me or something, mate?"

"No, no, I am just beatifically happy."

"You were pretty happy this morning as well."

"It's this new inner peace I've found."

"Well, I better not find you laughing at me next time I see you."

In Latin America, archaeologists point with great pride at the achievements of the Aztecs and the Incas, who built great cities and palaces yet were ignorant of the wheel. In a like vein, Australian sociologists might show pride in the smooth running of Australian society, a society where constant good humour is all but unknown.

Moodiness is also used in the family, generally on young impressionable children *before* their ability for even temper has been developed.

"Hi, mum! I'm home!"

"Oh. It's you."

"Sure it's me. Wait till I show you this!"

"Not now. I'm in a Bad Mood."

"Later then?"

"Let's just hope you're a good boy and don't upset me."

By this method, the child quickly learns that not only has moodiness the ability to instil guilt in the moodee (that is, the person being mooded upon) but that anything new or interesting or different should be met with a repertory of moods that will, hopefully, prevent others from persisting with their ideas, or asking for your help.

Should someone come out with something like "Hello, Jim, I've been meaning to talk to you seriously", the silly, incoherent mood of neurotic giggles ought to be called into action. Suddenly everything is amusing. Wave your arms madly and try to stop the other person from saying anything important.

If this does not work, it is advisable to act as if you can hardly remember anything. For this purpose, look fierce of frown. Grimaces achieved by stretching lips and baring teeth are also effective. Scratching parts of the body is good, but not the crotch area as it is too Mediterranean.

If still not successful, try the blank mood. This is a distracted gaze, one that implies both toothache and a case of mistaken identity.

Last resort: the punch-up, the ultimate Australian mood. What "the blues" are to American blacks, "world-sorrow" to Romantic poets, or "satori" to Zen Buddhists, the punch-up is to Australians. Its unexpectedness and general baselessness make it endearingly antipodean.

The phone

MOST of us employ much the same clouting techniques to recover unused coins from a broken public phone-box whether we are in Brisbane or Bombay, and it is no more aggravating trying to get through to a continually engaged number in Adelaide than in Addis Ababa. There are, however, a few specific local procedures which callers ought to be conversant with since methods pioneered here over the course of the past century have made telephoning in Australia a unique experience.

As a rule Australians are friendly and cheerful over the telephone. Unlike many overseas interlocutors they welcome your call and are happy to exchange views and information. The general awareness of good phone manners is extremely high, in line with the lofty scale of civilisation reached by the entire nation. It is virtually inconceivable not to want to do business with most Australians after the friendly reception they offer callers.

Australians are also invariably keen to postpone discussions or negotiations to a further date.

Your expected and traditional course of action is to:

Agree readily on a time and date at which they are going to ring you back; and then — Forget all about it. As soon as you hang up you must not expect to hear from them again.

After years of trial and error Australian business personnel in both private and public sectors have discovered that the real aim of the telephone is to inform callers in a friendly fashion that the person they are seeking is somewhere else. Furthermore it has been realised that if you make the whereabouts of the sought person a complete mystery then the chance of callers ever attempting to call again will be highly diminished.

"One moment please. That number is engaged. What? No, she's also gone to lunch. Who? Let me check. I'm sorry but he has gone to a meeting. I'll put you on to somebody else."

You are now talking to Somebody Else.

"I'm afraid this is not my department. Can you call later? Well, yes, I suppose I could ask. Look, why don't I transfer you and you can ask yourself."

The next person: "No, you've been wrongly transferred. I'll try to get you back to the switchboard. But I'm new here and it might take some time."

With adroit telephone management callers will either:

(a) give up in despair

(b) forget what they rang about in the first place.

Telephoning after hours is fine provided you keep in mind that most people will be nervous wrecks when answering your call as they tend to interpret the ringing to mean the following:

8-9 pm a personal crisis.

9-10 pm a family crisis.

10-11 pm a death in the family.

11-midnight World War III.

Phone calls after midnight can only mean one thing in Australia: someone's dialled the wrong number.

How to build on shaky foundations

O N the West Coast of America and in Japan they had to devise ways to construct buildings that could withstand the earthquakes that plague those regions. In Venice they had to devise ways to build elaborate streets and palaces on the marshy lands of the lagoon. In Australia, similarly, you must learn to build on shaky foundations.

Australia is a young and changing society and your foundations may not always be quite as steady as you would wish. Like in all such situations you have to tread very lightly, take wary steps, develop a brand new set of approaches and come up with a few lateral solutions. Here are some suggestions.

1 Make sure to get into a business you know nothing about. This way you won't be prejudiced by old-fashioned or outmoded ideas regarding what works and what doesn't. Stodgy and dull Europeans might argue and debate for years and sometimes even decades whether or not a particular scheme is feasible before embarking on it. Australians, by contrast, have abandoned the prejudices of the old world and are quite prepared to plunge into enterprises without a second glance.

2 Don't look into deals to see whether or not they are viable. Do things for the joy of it. Australians know that if you make too many enquiries before you commit yourself you might find out some unpleasant facts and be discouraged.

"It's a lovely house."

224

"Did you get a building report?"

"You can tell it's sound just by looking at it."

"Did you have a pest inspection done?"

"The people we're buying from assure us it isn't necessary."

"What about vacant possession?"

"The squatters promised to leave once we're ready to move in."

3 Be supremely confident about everything and explain that it is the only way to do things. Should you begin a new project, be excited about the outcome then pass the work on to someone else. This is called *knowing how to delegate*. Lose interest in projects just as they are about to reach completion. This is called *going on to bigger and better things*. Don't spend time consolidating plans, time is too valuable.

4 Highly ceremonious Asians will insist on meeting people under the most formal circumstances and then will only trust those recommended by people they've known since childhood. In Australia, however, you must be ready to drop all formality and feel quite happy to enter into partnership with people you ran into during your lunch break.

5 In Australia you will not get credit unless you are in debt. Make sure you never pay cash for anything. Keep tabs on all the people you owe money to and if necessary bring them in to your bank to act as witnesses. Make your motto: "Live for today — tomorrow you probably can't afford it."

The art of over-extending

THE national art in Switzerland is yodelling from great heights. In Hungary, painting colourful flower motifs on everything in sight. In Brazil, inventing ever-harder-to-remember dance steps. In Kenya, carving rows of ebony elephants linked trunk to tail.

In Australia the national art is over-extending yourself.

In countries such as China or Ethiopia, where over-population or war has produced a scarcity of food, the skill to use every edible scrap has become an art form. Similarly, in Australia, where savings are scarce, everyone has developed the art of borrowing on everything from last year's unsettled insurance claim to next year's anticipated tax-refund.

No matter what their income level, people in Australia are fully over-extended. The same zeal once used to colonise the continent, build the Indian-Pacific railway and irrigate vast tracts of land, is now applied to borrowing right across Australia from Abbotsford to Perth.

Talented and inventive, Australians have developed the art of over-extension with true pioneering gusto. Devotees of the craft, found throughout the continent from Darwin to Humpty Doo, have caught their strong aesthetic creed in the pithy saying:

"Why save when I can borrow?"

After all, saving can be tedious, time-consuming and full of effort, whereas borrowing, or rather over-extending yourself, has nothing but advantages:

1 You can afford an impressive life-style with a minimum of physical exertion.

2 You are certain to acquire exciting new friends as there are so many other people around in the same situation.

3 Your credit cards work everywhere and if they don't someone else's will.

Analogous to the great culinary masters of the East who can transform something as mundane as a carrot into a beautiful rose, the great Australian exponents of the art of over-extending yourself, whose mastery at borrowing merits them the title of Living National Treasures, have discovered ways of converting the smallest asset into a fabulous life-style.

"I decided to put a ten percent deposit on my new bachelor flat and then took out a second mortgage to pay for my overseas holidays."

"Well, I showed them my fishing gear and they lent me the money to buy a trawler."

Tried and true connoisseurs of the difficulties involved, Australians look up to those who have successfully over-extended themselves as much as the French esteem their philosophers and Russians worship their war-heroes. "One minute he was just this guy with a nine-to-five job and the next thing you know he had managed to borrow more than most people earn in a lifetime."

How to be a great negotiator

NEGOTIATING in other countries means wanting to get an advantage over your opponent. The Japanese may prolong discussions for three or four years over a simple point under the guise of wishing to make a unanimous decision. Russians make sure they appear virtually abuse-proof and will come back cheerfully no matter how many times they get knocked back. The French will wine and dine you until you are so softened up that all your will to fight has drained out of your fibres. The Americans will just want to bribe you, bribe your superiors, your superiors' superiors, your family, their families, everyone's in-laws and anyone who happens to be delivering the morning papers.

Australians, by contrast, have decided to cut all the crap.

In Australia, you see, you don't need any of these advantages over your opponent since you already have one by being Australian.

Make it clear right from the start that you are a great negotiator and that you never give an inch in any transaction. It will impress all those you don't have dealings with and will give fair warning to those with whom you do.

Develop a no-nonsense uncompromising attitude. Act tough and scowl a lot. Appear completely in charge of any situation you don't understand.

"I convened this meeting to discuss the situation."

"Sure."

"We want work bans on all existing delicatessens."

"If you wish."

"No deliveries of sausages, salamis or sauerkraut."

"Boy, did I go in there and give them something during those negotiations!"

"OK by us."

"Delighted to see you're taking such a sensible attitude."

"Actually we're here to remove all the old potplants."

Not only state up front what your demands are but also make sure you do it in a forthright aggressive manner while walking in through the door.

"We want $2.15 per item."

"Well..."

"And won't take anything under $2.10."

"But..."

"Unless you make a firm offer for $2.00."

Should you happen to negotiate with Greeks there's always a good chance that sometime between the start and close of proceedings they'll get up and announce that the whole process doesn't interest them anyway, they're sorry to have gotten into it in the first place, that it was a misunderstanding all along, they don't really wish to buy, sell or settle anything. This has a pretty poor effect on your self-confidence and soon you find yourself happy to agree to whatever they say.

The Chinese concept of negotiating takes a totally different course. To begin with they'll confess that their dearest wish is to make the decision in your favour but unfortunately the verdict never depends just on them, there are others to be considered too who haven't made up their minds yet and so they'll wear you down by coming back dozens of times to ascertain price, conditions or terms. The net effect of all this, especially when stretched over a few years, is to have you crawling for mercy.

Unlike these complex practices, the rules of Australian negotiating are simple and straightforward:

1 Being democratically-minded ensure that you never distinguish between underlings and people with real influence and power. Treat them all the same.

2 Be firm but in a vacillating uncertain sort of manner. State your demands up front in strong aggressive

tones, for instance, then look quickly around the room to see if you've done the right thing.

3 Do not forget that at the sign of slightest conflict, of angry words or bluffing outbreaks from your opponent, it is only sporting to give in and sign whatever paper they place in front of you.

4 Call whatever you end up with a great victory for common sense.

An alternative school of Australian negotiating states that it's probably best not to negotiate at all, to have nothing to do with one's opponents, rivals or competitors, that it's better to ignore them completely:

"No one tells us what to do" — except for the Americans, the Japanese, the Poms, the Indonesians, the IMF, the World Heritage Council, the World Bank, the Unions and the rich.

The art of the minuscule

Say a large crack appeared up the side of the building and the Body Corporate has been convened to see what can be done. Everybody gears up for a serious discussion on what to do about the crack in the wall.

In China you would attempt to find a solution by saying: "Comrades, according to the immutable laws of dialectic marxist-leninism, we should ferret out the class enemy saboteur responsible for this crack." In England you would most likely say: "I grew up in my great grandfather's house where a crack appeared in the building some two hundred and fifty years ago and the structure still isn't any the worse for it."

In Australia you focus instead on the non-essential non-specific feeling you have about the situation. In other words, you zero in on the minutia. Zoom in on the least important aspect of the situation. The most minuscule issue and one that is most easily overcome.

Devote your whole energies to it.

You don't do this because Australians are trivial-minded people. You do it in order to get control of the situation. Focusing on trivia proves that you are a serious, deep-thinking person whose sharp eye for detail intimates the thorough understanding you have of the whole though unstated process.

1. People come prepared with bits of paper. Someone has a quote from the best structural engineer. Someone else has a friend who is a builder and is willing to repair the building and guarantee the work. Another person got hold of the original architect who said he is willing to come out and supervise the repairs.

2. Someone is always sure to start the meeting with something intensely serious. They will come out with:

    "It's dangerous this crack. The draft's really coming through on all the floors."

    "Yeah, my father-in-law lives in a building and they have a large crack in their wall too."

    "Really? Isn't that funny, my mother-in-law has a large crack."

3. You yourself don't go prepared with technical knowledge about the causes of the crack because this would just bore everybody. It would present an unnecessary burden for them.

4. A lady will say: "I saw the crack appear last Thursday."

    "Oh, you are wrong there," you retort, "I think it was Wednesday."

    "Oh, no, no, I'm sure it was Thursday because I was out there watering the garden on Wednesday and there was no crack then."

    "You couldn't have watered the garden on Wednesday because it rained all day."

    "You're right! It must have been Tuesday."

    "Tuesday morning, to be exact," you answer. "I remember now because I noticed that the plants were really dry."

    Someone is sure to burst out enthusiastically at this point: "Yes, yes, we should put in an automatic sprinkler system!"

    "And we should plant more palms while we're at it!" you add.

You are now the authority of the situation and everyone's relieved because they don't have to make a decision about the crack.

The politics of politics

UNLIKE Britain, whose lengthy political history dictates perplexing bureaucratic structures, Australia's more recently created political system is easy to understand and simple to follow. There are nine houses of parliamentary assembly, eight non-federal houses of elected representatives, seven parliaments with upper and lower houses, six houses of elected senators, five influential parties, four arms of judiciary, three tiers of government, two branch levels to every party and one governor general.

This arrangement is, of course, not only simple and straightforward but also highly equitable to every Australian. Due to the small population of the country and the large number of politicians needed to fuel the system, your statistical chances of becoming elected, chosen, picked, designated, shanghaied, blackmailed, coaxed, nagged, plagued, irritated, exasperated or annoyed into seeking a position in Australian politics at some time or other in your life are greater than anywhere else in the world.

For this reason it's advisable to be mindful of the following basic fact.

Political parties in Brazil oppose each other in a seemingly brutish fashion. At election-time they go for the jugular without regard for truth or law; most parties grab what power they can and those that miss out retreat to plan either deadly juntas or lethal campaigns of vilification.

It couldn't happen in Australia.

Competition between opposing parties in India can become so intense and escalate to such a tumultuous

235

pitch that instead of candidates chasing the electors' votes it is the electorate that chases the candidates down the street armed with clubs and machetes.

It couldn't happen in Australia.

Party rivalries in Spain ended in civil war between the Falangists and the Republicans; in China, they culminated in an all out struggle between the Nationalists and the Communists; in Mexico, in a protracted war between the Conservative and the Revolutionary parties.

It couldn't happen in Australia.

Australians are careful to avoid civic conflict of any sort and are keen to see their various political parties coexisting in harmony with one another. They have agreed therefore that all political fighting should go on not between parties but *inside* them.

As in all democratic societies, this is done on a regular basis and with a high ratio of participation. Lying, cheating, back-stabbing, betrayal, treachery, disloyalty, subversion and perfidy are all used with great gusto.

Every party member thus gets a chance of a rounded view of politics and becomes familiar with the democratic political process. And since the parties are busy fighting within their own ranks they have no energy to carry out any major reforms, which means the country can remain stolid, stable and ever unchanging.

How to be the majority

IN China the majority are farm workers. In Brazil, the unemployed. In Bangladesh, flood victims. In Afghanistan, guerilla fighters. In Kuwait, rich idlers.

The majority in Australia are government employees.

Schools, universities, airlines and electricity, along with gas and water utilities, several banks, motor registries, the largest insurance companies, post offices, hospitals, libraries, trains, buses, trams, sewerage and garbage disposal services all belong to the state and are all staffed by government workers.

If you are lucky enough to be accepted into the wide ranks of Australia's local, state or federal public servants, you must be careful to uphold generations of tradition. Below are the basic attitudes you need to exhibit in order to fit happily into any of these organisations.

Remember — in the new public service there is no guaranteed tenure. This is why you must try so much harder.

1 The instant you walk in through the door of your place of employment each day, you must begin to:
   (a) look listless, care-worn and tired;
   (b) sigh;
   (c) groan.
An impression of permanent and irreversible exhaustion is the sign of true efficiency. It is the hallmark of the devoted, dutiful and hardworking Australian government employee. English public servants pretend to be efficient, Germans go for strictness, in India officiousness is probably the general rule. In Australia if you do not seem terminally tired, or

237

The world-famous Australian termite castles.

fatally buggered, you will simply not be taken seriously or respected by either your colleagues or the public at large.

2 Should you find yourself in a situation where your chief task is to deal with members of the general public, you must be careful to ensure that a long queue is formed at all times before anyone behind the counter resumes work. Bear in mind that Australians are a patient and well-behaved people. They never complain of having to queue up and wait since in the olden days whenever someone did speak out, everyone was punished. See how long you can hold them off. Make side bets with other employees.

3 As Australia is a vast country with a great future, you would be wise to plan carefully for long term periods. No matter which section of the public service employs you, map out your possible free days several years in advance. Outline exactly what days you will not be working on up to a decade at a time. Ensure you are always able somehow to get a day off whenever you want to. Organising flexie-time dates, preferably in massed clumps, is also a major duty. Plan sick leaves well ahead, giving special attention to synchronisation with annual and public holidays.

Whining and Dining

The whine

If you want to sound really and truly dignified, you must develop a whine in your voice.

Now, what is a whine?

The dictionary calls it a plaintive, high-pitched, protracted sound as in pain, fear, supplication or complaint. Because nature is the best teacher we have, I would define it as a cross between a hand-cranked siren and a lethargically strangled cat.

You could develop a whine like the Prime Minister which took him years to acquire and the people love him for it. They understand only too well that he, along with everyone else, has learnt in childhood that it is the only way anyone will listen and take notice of what you say.

Exercise before the mirror. Start by squinting the eyes. Next squint with your body. Practise a whole body squint. Now imagine yourself in Iraq, giving voice to a Bedouin love song.

A fine distinction must be made here. Having a whine in your voice is not the same as whingeing. Only the English may whinge, it is their prerogative. The best you can aim for is a lingering and distinguished whine.

How to say "No" to everything

You must learn to be against everything, because that is terribly Australian. All modern-thinking progressive Australians are opposed to change or anything new and are respected for it.

In fact, more Australians have put their names to petitions that were *against* new projects, developments, schemes or proposals than *for* them.

Occasionally there's trouble with overseas investors, bankers and architects who don't seem to understand that in Australia it is normal to be against: tall buildings, long bridges, tunnels, airplanes, airports, heliports, imports, exports, holiday resorts, strikes, strike-breakers, smoking, non-smoking, lopping down trees, putting up sports grounds, digging into the earth, damming up water, medical experiments, slow reactors, fast railways and modern inventions, since it shows that you are a serious person with deep committed feelings.

The fact that the country might go to pot as a result is simply irrelevant.

An advanced party of Australian Citizens Against Everything

State-of-the-art survival

Should you decide to become a purveyor of the Arts, it would be in your better interests to follow the basic rules that make entertainment in Australia both unique and peculiarly antipodean. Here are some suggestions.

1 Classical Drama
When presenting a classical play, you must change it beyond recognition, so as to cause the audience to wonder why on earth the work became famous in the first place. You must also call this new mess an "up-dated adaptation". It is quite acceptable to treat the author and the public as morons.

2 Classical Music
If possible, never tune a piano correctly for either concerts or recitals, in order to be able to test the musical sensibilities of the audience to the fullest. Also, overseas soloists should be instructed that the real purpose of applause in Australia is not to show appreciation but to see, as a matter of principle, just how many encores may be squeezed out of a jet-lagged and otherwise exhausted performer.

3 The Australian Film Industry
Every few decades, Australians like to get together and decide to have a film industry. This is necessary as all previous Australian efforts to make internationally successful films have had to be abandoned. The following are generally to blame: American distributors, greedy unions, the poms, the brain drain, lack of talent,

244

small budgets, big budgets, too many films, not enough films, poor scripts, too many producers, unscrupulous investors, public apathy, interference, rising wages and the falling dollar.

To the credit of the indomitable Australian spirit, film makers in this country just don't know when to give up.

4 Art Galleries
Art galleries should, as a rule, be situated in narrow, inaccessible lanes or built along busy clearways, a half hour's walk from the nearest parking. It is advisable to employ assistants who can make clients feel inferior and stupid. If such are unavailable, hire a pretty teenage boy.

Women are advised to run the arts

Why artists look like accountants

In Europe, successful artists are usually known for their colourful personalities. There was once a famous European playwright who lived well beyond his means. Every day, his creditors would clamour outside his door, demanding payment. To satisfy them, the playwright would once a year put the names of all his creditors in a hat, and draw out ten of them; only these ten would then get paid.

One particularly unlucky tradesman's name had failed to come up year after year. He became hysterical. "Sir!" he shouted. "If you cannot afford it, you shouldn't live in such luxury! I will cause a scandal!" The playwright, however, warned him with a stern voice: "Keep quiet, sir, or next time I won't even put your name in the hat!"

It couldn't happen in Australia.

Far from being extravagant and colourful, successful artists in Australia take pride in their frugality and ordinariness. My first encounter with one of the species was at a party.

"And who is that quiet little accountant in the corner?" I asked rather loudly of my hostess, finding out only too late that I had probably made an enemy for life of a well-known serious composer.

But to my surprise, I saw a slick of satisfaction spread across the man's face. Unknowingly, I had paid him a compliment. Later, I found out that the poor man had always felt that people did not consider him to be making an honest living. He therefore tried to seem as ordinary and as average as possible.

Very soon I learnt that Australians feel much more at ease with artists who not only have the appearance of accountants, but their regular habits as well. Rising early is *de rigueur,* eating toast with Vegemite a must; wearing terry-towelling hats to the footy or the cricket is essential.

For this reason, most successful people in the arts are careful to let it be known that being a creative person in Australia is really a nine-to-five job. They insist that these hours are the most inspirational, and that creating outside them is rather unprofessional. This relaxes everybody and reassures them that what artists are doing is in truth good, old-fashioned, hard sweat-of-the-brow type work.

Musicians like Mozart and Handel, or writers like Balzac and Dickens, working around the clock, managed to knock up whole operas or novels in a matter of days. They were guilty of amateurish and unprofessional methods simply not tolerated on the serious Australian creative scene. Not only were these artists too fast and unmindful of unionist work ethics, but to make matters worse, not one of them was ever known to mow his lawn, change the wheel of a carriage or belong to a baby-sitter club.

The grant system

The Grant System is designed to appeal to the innate gambling spirit of all Australians. Those who apply for grants understand intrinsically that their application is not much different from having a flutter on the horses or dogs.

But as the popular Australian saying goes, "You've got to be in it to win it". Therefore every month of an artist's year should represent the closing date of a particular government grant.

JANUARY — Special Purpose Grant
(Deceased Estate Auction: down payment on neglected three-storey block of flats)

FEBRUARY — Senior Fellowship Grant
(legal costs and stamp duty)

MARCH — Creative Development Grant
(new guttering and plumbing and a new section of roof)

APRIL — Script Assistance Grant
(re-carpeting of three-storey stairwell)

MAY — Overseas Research Grant
(light fittings and chandeliers to be bought in Hong Kong)

JUNE — Second Reassessment Grant
(pay accountant and sundries)

JULY   Federal Arts Award Grant
            (garbage disposal unit)

AUGUST   Multicultural Studies Grant
            (Italian marble for the hallway)

SEPTEMBER   Special Projects Grant
            (repair built-ins and furniture)

OCTOBER   Visual Arts Exchange Fellowship
            (repaint walls and make good)

NOVEMBER   Special Environmental Studies Grant
            (landscape back and front gardens)

DECEMBER   Overseas Study Tour Grant
            (down payment on the block of flats next
            door, then off on long deserved holiday)

When filling in grant forms, your stated aims must sound determined, idealistic and non-controversial. It would be helpful if you could prove that the project has already been successfully done overseas.

During the interview, you should appear relaxed, non-ambitious and friendly — in a frigid sort of a way, of course. If interviewers act too friendly you can be sure you missed out. It helps to have had an affair with one of the assessors first.

Once you have the money, immediately ask for a hefty extension of one or two years, "due to other commitments". Divorce is a good excuse for women. Having to look after the kids is the usual excuse for men.

After several such extensions, publish in a Saturday morning paper your reasons for not fulfilling your obligations to date, followed up by an attack on the whole Grant System. Then apply for a grant to research the state of the Arts in Australia, on the basis of your two-part newspaper article (second part of which, still incomplete).

Great inventions

AUSTRALIANS have proved to be the resourceful originators of many great scientific innovations. But while the brilliant minds that developed the Sarich Orbital Engine, In Vitro Fertilisation and Mixomatosis have received international accolades for their achievements, little or nothing has been heard of the imaginative Aussie brains who have taken on the challenge of inventing invisible diseases.

As supposedly advanced countries like the USA, Germany and Japan have virtually ignored this field, it has been left to Australia to shoulder the burden of carrying out the necessary research. Thanks to the effort of some of the nation's finest intellects, the country that gave the world the Plastic Downpipe and the Green Bean Slicer now provides everyone with equal and substantial opportunities to make it big in the field of compensation.

An arsenal of invisible diseases stands at your disposal: Kangaroo Paw, Mediterranean Back, Permanent Migraine, Gastro, Colic, Reflux, Colitis, RSI (Repetitive Strain Injury), TOAD (Tool Operating Allergy Distress) and Compensation Neurosis, to name but a few.

As a good Australian you can do your bit by inventing a new invisible disease. With luck you can build an entire career on this and even enter politics. With judicious approach you can perfect the technique of never having to work again.

Discoveries may come to the simplest of people, in the simplest of ways. You meet up with some old friends

Australian inventors await the judges' final decision.

who live in luxury houses and don't seem to work very hard. Five years before they were work-mates. Now you look around and ask in amazement:

"How did you do it? I haven't even been able to save a deposit on a bachelor flat."

"That's because you go about it the wrong way."

"What do you mean?"

One of your friends takes a step nearer: "Are you sure you're feeling OK?"

"Yeah," adds another, "it's pretty hazardous work you're doing."

"No, no, I'm just packing 250 gram tins into small boxes."

"I bet there's a lot of bending and lifting."

"No, they come along an assembly line and you just pick them up and plop them in. They've even supplied us with adjustable seating."

"Adjustable, eh?" muses someone.

"Yeah, these modern contraptions can be pretty dangerous," observes another.

"I heard lots of people get their fingers broken trying to move the seats up and down," says a third helpfully.

"No, no, it's all quite easy — they're on air-cushions and there's a lever."

"A lever!" says one meaningfully.

"A lever!" echoes another."And how many times a day do you have to bend down to move the lever?" asks the third.

Like Stevenson, Pasteur and Sarich, the inventor's inspiration strikes. "Geez, yes! What with the repetition of putting the cans into boxes and having to move the lever up and down all the time, I reckon it could be really bad for me!"

"That's right! Something like that happened to me!"

"And me!"

"And me!"

Congratulations all around.

Your friends are adamant. "Don't go into work any more until you fix the problem."

"But I need the job to pay my bills."

"No, mate, this is serious, what you need is to get on top of the situation. You're not within a cooee of working for the next five years."

Take note, however, that the precise guidelines set out by the ACA (Australian Compo Association) for such inventions are stringent and must be rigidly adhered to:

1 In the early stages the malady must be undetectable by scientific means yet must still qualify the sufferer to take a couple of hours off work each day.

2 As time passes the condition must not cause any serious pain to the claimant yet should appear severe enough to support a sizeable claim for compensation.

3 The illness should have a built-in deterioration factor so that after a few months of futile treatment, a year's time off from work on full pay is the only solution.

4 The ultimate test of a good disease is whether or not it can be eventually pronounced incurable. This will permit you to live on compo for the rest of your working life.

Getting on top of the Underdog

Australians are notorious for their sympathy with the Underdog. Far from being a mere figure of speech, the Underdog is as vital to modern day legends as the hero Siegfried was to Norse mythology. In fact, should anyone even so much as hint in passing at the word "Underdog", you must immediately chip in:

"Oh, I don't know, but I have this gut reaction to be on the side of the Underdog."

It's important to say this, because right away it will identify you as a person who:

1 Is not likely to rock the boat (only taking the side of a Tall Poppy would do that);

2 Is likely to lend money should the other person ask for it; and

3 Has no idea what they are talking about.

It also takes quite some time to realise that while you must always claim to take the side of the Underdog, you should never admit to being one. Do not be tempted to tell your audience, in the middle of a story:

"It was terrible — there we were fighting outside the pub, with a big crowd around us, and I was the Underdog."

Underdogginess, like being mauled by sharks, clearly happens only to other people.

The Dynamic Entrepreneur

AN education can be a severe handicap when it comes to making money. The Dynamic Entrepreneur has graduated from the school of hard knocks and draws on facts only if all else fails.

Ensure you don't have too many skills. They would only interfere with your infallible sense of always making the right choices.

Announce that money is not really important, it is merely the means to achieving a dream. And the dream is to become the richest person in Australia.

You have to be perpetually optimistic, especially when things aren't going too well: "Yeah, mate, future prospects are brilliant, the outlook is bloody outstanding. Timely actions taken in other places have really raised revenue expectations."

A modicum of down-to-earthness is highly recommended, because you have to demonstrate that the tedious vulgarities of income and social position have not spoilt you a whit. Uttering a few words such as *mate*, *dinkum*, *struth* as you are speeding away to an important meeting is considered unbelievably charming.

The Dynamic Entrepreneur is known for his outspoken, exacting attitude not only towards the truth but also towards those who might try to suppress it. Not for you the weak and ineffectual language used by everyone else.

"We bailed out of that project at least two and a half years ago to pursue other interests, as they say, but we

"Success! I now possess ten times my own body weight in debt!..."

are still trying to paper over the cracks and pull their hot chestnuts out of the fire."

The Dynamic Entrepreneur does not have any fixed long term plans because that would be "counter-productive." Go with the current. Roll with the punches. But whatever profits you do achieve, make it abundantly clear to everyone concerned that it was your intention to reach those targets all along.

Above everything, the Dynamic Entrepreneur is always right.

The bully

In most countries people are proud of their bullies and hold them up as national heroes. Germans admire nothing more than Beethoven's impossible temper. The British are prouder of their swaggering Henry VIII than of any other monarch. The domineering Morgan and Rockefeller are paragons of American business behaviour.

Don't expect to see it in Australia.

Here serious musicians are admired for their savourless character, Prime Ministers for their amicability and heads of corporations for their inoffensive blandness.

Successful people know never to attack anyone in public because Australians are fair-minded people who will automatically go to the defence of the person being aggressed.

This is the reason why wise politicians, sensitive artists and affluent business people in Australia know to shout only behind closed doors and then only at favourite family members, trusted colleagues, policy advisers and party underlings, who can be relied upon for masochistic discretion.

"What the hell do you think you're doing?"

"I thought I would bring the . . ."

"Don't you have anything better to do?"

"But you told me that . . ."

"Listen, mate, if I need a reminder I'll ring Telecom."

Abusing for hours on end faithful secretaries, cowed board-members is all right too, as long as you do it away

Public

from the limelight in sound-proofed rooms or in inaccessible offices.

"Whaaat the bloooody hell is thiiiis? What do you call these three green things in a box? Are you insane or something? Don't you every do that again! Jesus that bloody carrier is late again! I told him if he is not here by ten! Just bums! That's all I can get to work with! Nothing but bums!"

Try to sound angry and ready to explode at all times. Don't, for example, allow others to complete their sentences. Good Australians are carefully brought up by their fathers never to have the last word, so it ought to be plain sailing.

By contrast, your behaviour in public should always be unfailingly modest. Everyone's view is important. The little man or woman always gets a hearing. Do not put forward your own personal views in any discussion. Be like the Delphic oracle. Stand up for the rights of the

260

individual, preferably of those individuals you have never met in person.

"I respect everybody."

"Won't make up my mind until I hear all sides."

"The masses have the same rights as everyone else."

You shouldn't care, of course, about the opinions of those close to you, only about the fact that someone who has met the sister of the store manager whose driver delivers your groceries should go on saying things about you such as:

"You couldn't find a nicer bloke."

"She's a true lady."

"What a terrifically democratic person."

Private

Half mum, half management.

The role model

THE Role Model is often found in the area of public relations, media and fashion. A blondish shade of hair is desirable. It's good to have been married. Twice is even better.

The Role Model has the ability to do everything. You can bring up children, be an effective wife, have several successful careers in your lifetime, act as a socially responsible person, become the supporter of important charities. Nobody knows how the Role Model copes with her busy schedule, not even she.

The Role Model's aim in life is to fulfill her needs, wants, desires, ambitions and aspirations as well as strive for spiritual self-realization. In an ordinary person such a variety of goals might lead to emotional conflict and physical exhaustion, but these things do not affect the Role Model. You can be running a high-fashion company and advertise tent-frocks at the same time.

The only conflict the Role Model ever has is not with people but with issues. With people, you may have misunderstandings or cooling off periods, you may choose to go your separate ways or progress to maturer things, but ultimately you are certain that everyone deep down still loves and admires you. With issues it is a different matter. Here you may be as aggressive and stony as you like. Stopping tall buildings or tree felling are perfectly acceptable ways of expressing your aggression.

Whatever the average person achieves is always done with the help of others. The Role Model seems to be able to achieve most things on her own.

The Role Model is also multifaceted. Manifest a sense of humour about everything except yourself. Declare that the purpose of a woman's life is to:

(a) Teach men a lesson, that is be on two committees more than you have time for.

(b) Be a role model to women, in other words someone who no matter how busy she is still thinks of her family's breakfast.

You have to cultivate your reputation with the greatest care. The people surrounding you are always ideal and what imperfections they might manifest such as drug-addiction, alcohol dependency, nervous disorders or depression, have proved to be blessings in disguise by turning you into a stronger person and teaching you how to cope with the difficulties that crop up in your career.

How to be the minority

AUSTRALIA is, without doubt, the most egalitarian country in the Western World. Social distinctions are virtually nonexistent. Ninety-eight per cent of the population considers itself no better or worse than anyone else and is perfectly happy to live assimilated into the homogenous equality-minded community.

Unfortunately, there remains a misguided minority that seems unable to fit into the general populace. Due to a variety of historical reasons its members are unwilling to fit in and choose to live in small ghettos around the country.

If you want to make it really big in Australia you must pass yourself off as a member of this minority. It's both advantageous and profitable to be accepted as one of them because of the amount of preferential treatment and government assistance given to you if you do. Here are some notes on their background:

- It's estimated that they make up two per cent of the population. Many believe that Australia actually belongs to them. Others are convinced that the country is where it is today only because of the personal sacrifices made by members of this minority.

- Most are nomadic and have to commute between multiple dwellings. When the urge comes over them they throw everything down and follow a compulsion to travel long distances, often just for a few days.

• In the old days most were made to feel ashamed of their ways, with many forced to pass themselves off as average Australians. Of course, in trying to integrate into the rest of society they often lost their identity and, sadly, much of their self-respect.

Following much international criticism, however, society at large now bends over backwards to grant as much help to this minority group as possible. The government has come to realise that just because this small percentage of the population happens to own more than sixty per cent of the nation's wealth, it doesn't mean that they should be discriminated against.

Several important steps have been taken therefore by the various governments of Australia to improve the situation of this hitherto neglected group:

1 Considerable sums of public funds, increased Commonwealth aid and assistance programmes are being deployed to improve their life-style even further. Bigger homes, larger tennis courts, helipads and several other essential features such as servants (called "staff" to please Australian democratic sensibilities) are being accorded to them in an effort to keep them happy.

2 Fortunately the government has had the intelligence to legally protect the minority's interests by passing special legislation to change old-fashioned laws that say you can't own everything.

3 Moves towards giving them extensive privileges including rights to all natural resources, crown lands, media, railroads, airlines, forests, lakes, mountains and ocean foreshores are currently under way.

What is a Tall Poppy?

The ancient Greeks used to say that before the gods destroyed a man, they gave him everything. In a like vein, "Tall Poppy" is the designation Australians give their more successful enemies, just before attempting to destroy them.

You will hear a lot about Tall Poppies. All sorts of people will tell you that Tall Poppies, on the whole, are disliked, and that people turn against those who rise too high above others. Of course, being "poppies" they can only be a bit taller than the rest in the field. This is some comfort, perhaps, but of no consequence whatsoever to the "great Australian levellers".*

You mustn't, however, expect to meet anyone who actually admits to a personal dislike of Tall Poppies. By a strange quirk of circumstances, it seems that it is always the "jealous masses" who dislike Tall Poppies, never the speakers themselves.

As no one has ever come out publicly against Tall Poppies, their general characteristics can only be guessed at. Here are a few I have managed to ascertain:

1　Tall Poppies are just like you and me only more so.

2　They're usually below average height. This reputedly drives them harder.

3　They never live overseas. If they did they would be known instead as Successes — providing, of course, that they still call Australia "home".

A Tall Poppy Squad at work

Epilogue

An Australian preparing for life:

ROBERT TREBORLANG

Known for his best-selling books *How to Survive Australia, How to be Normal in Australia, How to Make it Big in Australia,* Robert Treborlang has also written plays, directed and produced documentaries, published articles on personalities, music and travel. Born in Jerusalem, carried off in childhood to Romania and then to France, he first came to Australia in his teens and has drawn inspiration from the place ever since.

MARK KNIGHT

Mark Knight has commented on subjects from the Australian economy to the personalities of politicians in the national press. He began his career with the *Sydney Morning Herald,* later became political cartoonist for the *Australian Financial Review,* and is currently the editorial cartoonist on the Melbourne *Herald Sun.* He is the author of several books of drawings, among them *Knight's Day* and *Having a Nice Day in America.*